Scars & Stripes

Hope for adult children of alcoholic families

by

Roy H. Cantrell

Published by Waldenhouse Publishers, Inc.
Walden, Tennessee

About the cover: Roy H. Cantrell as a youngster is pictured against the sun, a symbol of hope, rising over the Appalachian mountains. Cover photo by Charlie Stone.

Scars & Stripes:
Hope for adult children of alcoholic families

Copyright 2005 by Roy H. Cantrell
All rights reserved

Waldenhouse Publishers, Inc.
100 Clegg Street, Walden (Signal Mt.), Tennessee USA 37377
888-222-8228   www.waldenhouse.com
Printed in the United States of America
Library of Congress Cataloging-in-Publication Data

Cantrell, Roy H. (Roy Harold), 1939-
  Scars & stripes : hope for adult children of alcoholic families / by Roy H. Cantrell.
     p. cm.
  Summary: "Pastor Cantrell's stories of his youth in the 1940's in the coal mining regions of West Virginia and Kentucky explain how, with help from a Christian mother, he and his siblings coped with an alcoholic father. The narrative is intended to offer hope to adult children of alcoholic families"--Provided by publisher.
  ISBN-13: 978-0-9761033-2-5 (alk. paper)
  ISBN-10: 0-9761033-2-X (alk. paper)
  1. Adult children of alcoholics--Psychology. 2. Adult children of alcoholics--Religious life. 3. Alcoholics--Family relationships.
4. Self-realization. I. Title: Scars and stripes. II. Title.
  HV5132.C36 2005
  362.292'4'092--dc22

                                    2005022923

Special Tribute

⫷◆⫸

There is no one I love and respect more than my faithful and brilliant wife, Kaye. She has the wisdom of Solomon, and the healing touch of an angel. My faithful companion of 44 years, my best friend. A gift from God!

Ina Kaye Cantrell

This book is affectionately dedicated to my godly mother.

Easter Cantrell as a young mother photographed at the age of 21

Easter Cantrell upon earning her bachelor's degree in theology

Acknowledgements

There are a number of people I would like to thank for their contribution to my book.

- I am deeply grateful to my wife, Kaye for her incredible support and belief in me.

- I would like to express my appreciation to Becky Ostrzychi, Mary Lee Gwinnip, and Debbie Wittman who have proofread these materials. A special thanks to Joan Mahoney for her constant encouragement. I would also like to express my appreciation to my brother, Michael, who did research of our family genealogy and for his marketing advice.

- A special thanks to City Gate Church and Lecretia Everett, director of the prayer team, for their untiring prayer support, without whom this book would not be in print.

- Last, but not least, eternal gratitude to My Heaven Father for His unconditional love toward me, and for calling me into the ministry in spite of my imperfections and scars.

The Cantrell Team: Karen, Kaye, Roy (Howie), and yours truly. Kaye and I,have two incredibly gifted children. They are powerfully anointed servants of God. We are blessed!

Introduction

⟫⬧⟪

MY PURPOSE in writing *Scars and Stripes* is to raise awareness of the importance of working through one's pains. I have waited for over a half of a century to tell my story. I needed this time to work through the process of making peace with my own painful past so that I can guide others down the path of healing.

I realize there is a danger in looking back to the past. Paul says in Philippians 3:13-14, " ...this one thing I do, forgetting those things which are behind, and reaching forth unto those things which are before, I press toward the mark for the prize of the high calling of God in Christ Jesus."

On the other hand, I believe there is value in seeing your life in retrospect. It can help, and many time force, you to move beyond the bondage and codependency of those past years and bring you to the place where you are able to give God the glory. A glance backward should only be a temporary phase in the process of healing so that you are then able to press onward toward the future.

Years ago I heard a story that has stuck with me through its analogy. There was a little boy with a bad temper who flew off in a rage at the slightest provocation. His father wanted to help him learn the danger of his actions. His father gave him a bag of nails and told him to hammer a nail in the barn every time he lost his temper.

The very first day the boy drove 37 nails into the boards of the barn. With each passing day, the number grew less and less. Finally, the day came when the boy did not lose his temper at all. No nails had to be driven into the barn's walls. He was very excited and ran to tell his father of his progress.

His father instructed him that since he had reached this point, he could now pull the nails out one by one for each day he was able to control his temper. The days passed, and finally the young boy was able to report that the nails were gone.

The father took him by the hand and led him to the barn. He said, "You have done well, my son, but look at the holes in the barn. The barn will never be the same. When you say things in anger, those words leave a scar, just as the nails have in the barn. You can say 'I'm sorry,' but the wounds will still be there. A verbal wound is as bad as a physical one."

As I remember this story, I think of the carpenter who lived 2000 years ago in a little town called Nazareth who could plane the soul smooth, fill up the emotional holes of unmet needs, unhealed hurts and unresolved issues with the cement of His grace, and so paint us with the Crimson Blood of Calvary, that someone meeting us in heaven would never know that we had any scares at all. His name is Jesus.

He was wounded for our transgressions; he was bruised for our iniquities: the chastisement of our peace was upon him; and with his **stripes** we are healed. (Isaiah 53:5)

Praise the Lord!

Roy H. Cantrell, Ph.D.

Contents

My Heritage

EVERYONE HAS A physical and spiritual heritage that can be traced with the aid of a family tree. We've possibly all heard a lot about our flesh and blood ancestry, but normally we don't hear much about the spiritual ones. The latter is the most important.

I have always been interested in who my ancestors were, but I never spent the time doing an extensive search of my background, physical or spiritual. Most of the knowledge of my family history comes from my parents' reading me the names on the tombstones at our family cemetery when someone died, explaining who they were. I loved history, and this always made me feel more a part of them. But when they told me stories about those relatives who believed in God, my ears really perked up. Those interested me the most.

Just so you know a little more about me. I'd like to just take the time to introduce you to my immediate family: THE CANTRELLS

- My father: James Allen Cantrell (born March 11, 1915. Died August 7, 1992)
- My mother: Easter (Potter) Cantrell (born April 8, 1921)

• My siblings (in order of birth)

1. Roy H. Cantrell (that's me); (born August 22, 1939)
2. Kate Marie (born February 4, 1942)
3. Dora Lea (born May 4, 1944)
4. Zetta Lovern (born June 11, 1946)
5. James Allen (Junior: born June 28, 1948. Died November 11, 1951)
6. Novella Louise (born August 21, 1950)
7. Auldin Blain (born February 11, 1952)
8. Michael Dante (born September 26, 1957)

We lived in a coal mining camp called Second Bottom in a little community named Newhall, West Virginia. Dad moved there with the family from Pike County, Kentucky, 120 miles away, to find work in the coal mines, but we considered Kentucky our home.

The coal mining camps were close-knit communities. They were made up of coal miners and their families from various ethnic backgrounds. The cookie-cutter houses were built by the company, and the miners were charged rent. The coal company kept up the houses for a small fee until there was no more coal to mine. Then they sold them to the families at an exaggerated price.

Most of the houses soon deteriorated because there was no more money to keep them repaired. The younger generation soon moved away to look for jobs in the cities of Cleveland and Dayton, Ohio, and Detroit, Michigan, or some other city where a family member had migrated. Everyone in the coal camps looked out for each, though, and shared their food, money transportation, hand-me-down clothes, troubles and corn whiskey.

I can honestly say that Dad was a wonderful father when he was sober. He worked hard in the coal mines to provide for the family, but his alcoholic addiction caused him to live a Jekyll and Hide life. He had high morals when he was sober, and would correct us if we did anything wrong. However, when he got drunk, there wasn't anything he wouldn't do. When he sobered up, he would be embarrassed over his behavior and swore that he would never drink again. (Proverbs 23:29-35) The only problem was he was true to the scripture. Though he would not want to repeat his actions, he seemed unable to keep himself from doing so.

I often wondered if someone had not hurt him very badly when he was a boy, because hurt people tend to hurt people in return. Under the influence of alcohol, he was as cruel as anyone I ever knew. He would be just as mean to an animal as to a person for no reason at all. It didn't matter. When he was drunk, someone or something was going to experience pain from his hand. I would add here that not all alcoholic parents are violent and abusive; unfortunately, our dad was.

When I was a small lad, I used to enjoy sitting around the fireplace and listening to stories of our ancestors who had come from far away lands called England, France and Ireland. They came without anything and settled in the rugged mountains of the Appalachian Plateau.

One of my favorite mountaineers was Daniel Boone, who explored the wilderness around where I lived. I would hug up close to my mother as they told how he fought the Indians and how he killed bears, panthers and other wild animals.

The story that held the most intrigue for me was that of my great, great great-grandfather, whose name was Abraham

Cantrell, Sr. He was named after Abraham in the Bible who was a man of great faith (Hebrews 11:8-13).

Abraham Cantrell was born 1774 and died in 1858 at 84 years of age. I don't remember seeing a picture of him, but his faith in God was outstanding. He was a devout man of God, and a believer in miracles. He was a Baptist minister according to the 1850 Pike County, Kentucky Federal Census. There were no automobiles in his time, so he walked or rode a mule or horse to get to his assignments. The faith he had in God was no less spectacular than the other great men of his time such as Smith Wigglesworth and John Wesley.

On one of his assignments someone accompanied him. They came to a place where they should have been able to cross the river on a foot long. However, it had been washed away through a flood, and the river was still rising and made it impossible to cross. They had no means of cutting down a tree to make another foot log, so great, great, great-Grandfather decided to ask God to cause a tree to fall across the river. He did, and they were able to walk across it to the other side and continue on their journey.

At another time, great, great great-Grandfather and his son Abraham, Jr. became hungry as they were making their way to his preaching assignment. They spotted a "bee tree." A steady stream of bees was flying in and out of a knothole high in the tree, but it was too far up for them to climb to retrieve honey. So, again my great, great, great grandfather resorted to prayer. He told God that they would not take more from the hive than they could eat.

The same thing happened to this tree as it did with the one that produced the foot log. Through prayer alone, the tree fell to the ground and split wide open revealing the honey. The son traveling with him began to gather more honey into large popular tree leaves to take with him. When my great, great, great, grandfather saw what he was doing, he stopped him and reminded him that they had asked God for only enough honey for one meal. They left the remaining honey for the bees.

I believe these stories are true, and I'm glad that I had a great, great, great, grandfather who believed in God for great miracles. They have built my faith in just hearing about them. He was so dedicated to God and the Bible that he named his son, Abraham, Jr. He in turn named his son, Isaac. Isaac named his son Isaac Nelson Cantrell who was my Grandfather. They revered Abraham and Isaac so much they named four generations after them.

My desire, therefore, is to carry on the spiritual legacy of my ancestry. To do so, it takes more than just being a name on a family tree on a piece of paper. It takes being an example that will result in God's favor. The Scripture reveals a man such as that and it says, "And he shall be like a tree planted by the rivers of water, that bring forth his fruit in his season; his leaf also shall not wither; and whatsoever he doeth shall prosper." (Psalm 1:3) I WANT TO BE THAT MAN!

Grandparents of Roy Cantrell

Isaac Cantrell

Dora Cantrell

Ira Potter

Kate Potter

"Let's Shake On It"

THERE WAS A TIME when a handshake was as binding as any written contract.

My mother is eighty-four years old now, and she shared with me how she and Dad got engaged. Dad died in 1992, from mostly black lung which is a coal miner disease caused by inhaling coal and rock dust. Dad and Mother were raised just a few miles apart in the mountains of Eastern, Kentucky, and close enough to spark.

Their engagement came about in a strange way. It started with a chimney fire that burnt a hole in the wood shingles of my grandpa's house. Both of the young people ended up repairing the damage, but it was the sparks that flew between the two of them that started a fire that even her Pa could not put out.

'Pa was not fond of any boys who "came a courting" his girls He would not hesitate to chase off any young man whose intention was to marry. His objection to a marriage was more for fear of loosing a hand in the corn fields than anything else. He actually ran Dad off just prior to the fire and told him never to come back again, but then 'Pa invited him to return to fix the chimney and roof because Dad was a good carpenter. Big mistake!

Mother's job was to carry clay and wood shingles up the ladder into the loft and then hand them up to Dad through the hole in the roof where the fire had burned through. Dad and Mother had been flirting a little with a wink and a nod here and there when no one was looking, but they had never even kissed, let alone spoken of engagement. Mother would not admit it, but I believe she arranged the ladder detail so that she could get close to Dad. At any rate, 'Pa was away on business the day that Cupid shot his arrow.

'Pa stayed gone a lot because he made a living in those days trading livestock, swapping knives and selling moonshine at a road intersection called Shelby Gap. His absence gave Dad a perfect opportunity to make his move. As the old saying goes, "When the cat is away the mice will play."

Imagine this. Dad is on top of the house fixing the chimney when Mother makes the next trip up the ladder into the loft with a load of clay. She lifts the clay up to Dad and he sets the clay on top of the roof. This is the moment Dad has been waiting for, so he blurts out, "Easter, I won't go with anyone else if you won't." And mother replies, "Okay, Allen." Then Dad extends his hand down through the hole in the roof and says, "Let's shake on it." Mother reaches up and shakes his hand. On the gesture of a handshake they become engaged.

When Mother told me how she and Dad got engaged by shaking hands, it made me think about Michelangelo's "Creation of Adam" painting on the central ceiling of the Sistine Chapel in Rome. The painting portrays God reaching out to touch Adam's finger, through which the breath of God is transmitted. The painting is breathtaking, but for me the image of those two hands of Mom and Dad reaching out to each other through the hole in Pa's roof, though they were soiled with clay that day, is more precious to me than any famous work of art.

I don't know of anything else that has impacted my life as much as learning about the integrity Mom and Dad displayed during their courtship days. To learn about their respect for each other and commitment to purity before marriage makes me proud to be their son. I'm glad they shook on it!

Note: The day they shook hands, Mother was seventeen as of April 8th, and Dad was twenty two as of March 11th. They married May 12, 1938. They celebrated their 53rd anniversary in May 1991, and Dad died of black lung disease August 7th of that year at the age of 77.

Easter Potter Cantrell as a young woman

James Allen Cantrell as a young man

"Son, Your Crime Is For Whiskey"

By James Allen Cantrell

The following song was composed by my father while he was in the Chillicothe, Ohio penitentiary for moonshine whiskey. He was given one year and a day. When the "and a day" was added to a sentence, it meant that the entire time had to be served. However, Mother wrote the president, the governor, and the warden asking them to release him. Six months into his sentence, he was paroled. The day he was released, he came home drinking. I was twenty months old, and Mother and I had just gotten over the measles.

It was on a Wednesday evening just about the hour of three,
when the law came up in the mountain, they had a warrant for me.

They took me down to Pikeville, a little town you all know well;
they took their handcuffs off me and locked me up in their jail.

Before the judge I did plead guilty, these words I heard him say,
"Now, Son, your crime is for whiskey, I'll give you one year and a day."

Then they took me to Ohio, a place I had never been;
they took their handcuffs off me, and locked me up in the pen.

The questions they asked me 10,000, not a one now do I know,
but it took some preaching and praying before I made parole.

Note: Dad worked in the chair factory while in prison for four cents per hour. He sent mother $2.79, each month, and kept the rest for his expenses. Dad went to the third grade in school and could read a little by sounding out each word aloud, but he could not write. A man named Rosenburough wrote Dad's letter for him while he was in prison. Mother did not know that Dad could not write when they got married. Therefore, she thought the letter she received from prison were actually from him. The family has no record of anything written in Dad's own handwriting. The song he composed was committed to memory, and he sang it often when he was drinking. It had a sad funeral dirge sound to it.

Moonshining: Normal Way of Life

ONE OF MY EARLIEST BIRTHDAY PRESENTS was a model of a "moonshine still." Making moonshine was a "normal" way of life in the mountains of Eastern Kentucky. There were only two professions offered to a young man for earning money: "moonshining" or coal mining. Both were deadly.

My feelings at the moment when my father presented this gift to me are still fresh in my mind. Even though I was young, I knew that moonshine was important to our family's existence. My father had a huge smile of accomplishment and satisfaction on his face when he handed the heirloom to me. I don't think Colonel Sanders was any prouder in passing his secret recipe of Kentucky Fried Chicken to his heirs, than my father was of passing to me his recipe for making moonshine. It was all in keeping with the tradition of past generations.

I was proud to be the owner of such a precious toy but even more proud for what it represented. I was on my way to manhood! Besides that, the liquor served as a medicine, much like a sedative, a septic, and a cure for colds. I remember sipping a "hot toddy," made of moonshine whiskey with sugar and ginger when I was a child. I guess Mother though using it for medicinal purposes was okay, since I Timothy 5:23 states, "Use a little wine for the stomach's sake and for your often infirmities." Dad, on the other hand, stretched that verse out of proportion.

In order to earn money to go to the movies, I would fish whiskey bottles from the river when it flooded. Moonshiners were willing to pay five cents for each bottle. To catch the bottles, I attached a net to a long pole, stood on a bridge, and snatched them from the river as they floated by.

I was told that, in an attempt to stop the proliferation and the reuse of whiskey bottles, the government placed a coin in each bottle of "legal government bottled and bonded whiskey." It was usually a 50 cent piece or more, depending on the size of the bottle. The purchaser had to pay the value of the coin in addition to the price of the liquor. The purchaser was therefore motivated to break the bottle in order to get the coin, and that prevented the bottle from being recycled and reused. As an alternative, the bottle could be returned to the store for the worth of the coin inside. The government would then recycle the bottle and, either way, keep it out of the hands of the moonshiners.

It was a real dilemma for mountain people when they were not able to make and deal moonshine. Making whiskey to drink and sell was a lucrative business until the government put a stop to it. Although the mountain people respected the government, they couldn't understand why their livelihood was taken away. It created a hardship because they had few other ways to make a living.

Mountain people are God-fearing people, and they didn't want to break the law. Also preachers were preaching against moonshine, and to go against them was to go against God.

There was evident damage caused by liquor's effects on users. Moonshine brought horrible devastation in its wake — incest, physical and emotional abuse, poverty, and even worse, death. An alcoholic might be willing to sell or pawn his own soul for a drink of whiskey. They were willing to face the shame afterwards when they sobered up after learning what they had done while under its influence. They seldom remembered.

Just a few of the dastardly outcomes were:

• My grandfather shot two men (that I know of) and killed one of them. He spent six months in the local jail for his crime.

• My father was shot by his cousin who was under the influence of alcohol. The bullet went through his thigh, but missed the bone or he might have been crippled for the rest of his life.

• My uncle was shot and killed over a minor dispute.

• Another uncle who was drunk shot and killed a young boy he met on the road because the boy refused to give him the moonshine he was carrying home to his father.

• Many of the deaths in a town only 30 miles away called "Bloody Harlan" were caused by "white lightening."

Even though drunkenness, with its poverty, abuse, killings, and estrangement, ran rampant among families and friends, moonshine was still considered a necessary evil.

My grandmother told me that the only time she came close to sinning was when she and Grandpa went in debt for a house and several acres to raise their family. They didn't have any way to pay the debt, except to sell moonshine. She made a deal with God that if He helped her sell enough moonshine to pay off the $1200.00 debt, she would not sell another drop as long as she lived.

Sure enough, after the "home place" was paid for, Grandpa sent a man to Grandma to buy some moonshine. She told the man that she didn't have any. When he went back and told Grandpa what she said, Grandpa was furious.

He was steaming when he went back home and screamed, "What do you mean telling that man you didn't have any whiskey? You know we have plenty."

With her hands sternly placed on her hips, she replied, "You may have plenty, but I don't have any. Do you remember that I told you when we sold enough to pay off this place that I wouldn't sell any more? Well, we paid the last payment, and I am not selling it again."

Grandpa never asked her to sell another drop of the moonshine.

The marvelous hand of God led me out of a life of being involved with the profession of the mountain folk and kept me from the evils of making and selling moonshine. In turn, the tradition of passing on a moonshine still to my children was broken. Instead, I was able to tell them about the wondrous love or our Lord and Savior, Jesus Christ, who is able to protect, guide, and lead them in this life, and then bring them to Glory. I continue to praise Him for His guidance and leadership in our pilgrim journey here on earth.

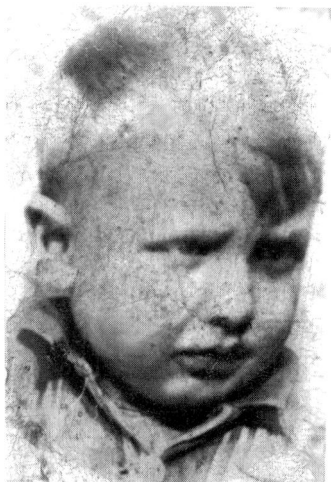

Roy Cantrell at about 12 months, just before his father went to prison.

Picture-In-The-Sky

MY FIRST ENCOUNTER with the supernatural happened when I was four years old. I can remember many details of that memorable day. The sun was bright and there was not a cloud in the sky. Our house was made of logs with two room, one for sleeping and the other for cooking, eating and entertaining (mostly family members). The windows were just holes sawed in the log walls and encased with rough lumber, hand hewn, and with hand made wooden shutters that was closed at night or when it was raining. Even though the house was very primitive, it was home to four of us. There was my father, Allen, and my mother, Easter, (I always loved her name), and my younger sister, Kate, and of course me.

The warm, peaceful day was interrupted by my mother's excited but slightly shushed voice calling my father's name to come and see what she was looking at from the back doorway of the log cabin. "Allen," she said, "come here and look at this." My father peered out of the open window located at the right side of the cabin door, and I ran to my mother's side and looked directly up into the cloudless blue sky. It was not unusual back in those days for someone to point out even a lone airplane flying over. That's what I though my parents were looking at. But there was no airplane that day. What were my parents looking at?

Suddenly, there appeared a window in the heavens. It was not the typical window that slides up and down vertically, but this one was horizontal; it slid from side to side. My grandmother had a window like this in the dining room of her house.

Then, I saw people dressed in waiter type clothes moving from table to table placing items here and there. They moved about as if they had to meet an imminent deadline for some grand event. I have never been able to describe the type of movement of the people. They moved with such ease, instantly located in one place and then another without appearing to be in a rush.

The rows of tables were as far as the eye could see, disappearing into the distance to a point much like rows of corn in an Iowa corn field. Not long ago I was in a Christian Bookstore and saw a painting that depicted the Last Supper, and it was almost identical to what I saw (except for the people).

The central focus in the picture was the appearance of a woman who entered the scene from the right side of the window. She was as large as life and was carrying a food tray in her hands. I couldn't see what was on the tray because the frame of the window cut off the view just below her elbows, but my impression was that it was some kind of food that had been prepared for the banquet. Her hair was shoulder length, and her movement was the same as the others. She turned and looked down in our general direction.

The whole drama lasted no more than a minute or two. All the time I am watching the scene unfold in heaven, my parents were oooohing and aaaahing at what they saw.

It wasn't until I was about 10 or 12 years old when I discovered we had not viewed the same thing. We were visiting my aunt Cassie in Neon, Kentucky. My mother had come to town to do some shopping. Of course all the children were left at home alone, and we loved the time away from the scrutiny of our parents. We didn't have television or electronic games to play, so we made up stories to tell. Story telling was a big thing when we were children, especially, "scary" ones. These "tales" were passed down from generation to generation. They were a great form of entertainment and if the "tale" was scary, it kept the children quiet.

When my turn came to tell my favorite scary "tale" I shared the "picture in the sky" I had seen when I was a child. When I finished, the unexpected happened. My cousins began making fun of my story and accused me of lying and threatened to tell my mother. I swore to them that I was telling the truth, but they would not believe me.

My defense was that I could prove my story was true by my mother because she had seen the same thing. In fact, she was the one who had shown me "the picture in the sky."

When Mother and Aunt Cassie returned home from shopping, my cousins ran immediately to my mother and ask her if we had seen a "picture in the sky" when I was a little boy. Their question shocked her, and her answer shocked me. She denied that she had seen anything and threatened to punish me for lying — to the delight of my cousins.

I began to cry and explain to her that she must have seen the "picture in the sky" because she was the one who showed it to Dad and me. I explained the event in such detail that she listened to me and then she remembered the incident. She became very serious and even turned a little pale (mountain people have a high regard for God) and began to explain what she saw that day.

A hen with several little chicks behind her was coming down the mountainside. Mother said the reason she was so excited was because the hen belonged to her mother had been missing for weeks. Her mother though that a fox had caught the hen. I never saw the hen and chicks. In retrospect, God had used the hen and chicks to get my mothers' attention so that He could get my attention.

I have tried to find some interpretation of the "vision" I saw. The closest I can come to its meaning is the reference to the marriage supper of the Lamb in the book of Revelation. I believe the woman in the vision was my Grandmother Dora (See *Grandma Dora's Baptism*.) Furthermore I believe it was given to me for encouragement ,because it has been something I have never forgotten and has lifted my spirits many times since the first day I got saved.

Approximately fifteen years later, I received Christ into my heart. I became discouraged and felt like quitting. I remember it well. I was cutting grass in a ditch along side our house with a hand cycle. My mind was bombarded with negative thoughts about whether there was a God. Dad had just sold my dog. (See *Ole Rowdy*.)

"There is no God and you're crazy for giving up all the pleasures of life for someone who doesn't exist," the voice said in my head. Then, I remembered the vision I saw when I was a child and I said out loud, "Yes, there is a God because I have seen into His heaven." The negative thoughts left immediately and I began to understand where those bad thoughts were coming from – Satan. If there was a Satan, then there must be a God, I reasoned.

Postscript: One of our grandsons saw a similar vision. One day while he was playing in the yard, he said to his father, "Dad do you see the pretty woman in the sky? Our son quizzed him about what he was seeing, and he was describing something in the heavens similar to what I had seen. Trey was no more than four years old at the time. He had never heard about my story.

The author at about age 6, two years after he had seen the "Picture In The Sky." At the same age he was photographed with his classmates at school, page 46.

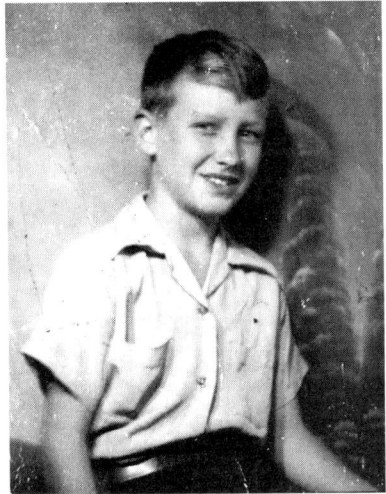

The author at about age 10 when he shared the story about the "Picture In The Sky" with his unbelieving cousins.

Allen and Easter Cantrell near their home in West Virginia.

New Shoes

⟨⬦⟩

I WAS BORN DURING the time of the Great Depression and World War II in the coal fields of Eastern Kentucky, and times were hard. They were doubly hard for those of us who lived on the Appalachia Plateau.

Coal mining was the main industry in those days in the Appalachian regions of Kentucky, Tennessee, Virginia, West Virginia and the Carolinas. The miners worked long hours in very dangerous conditions. It was not unusual for children to barely know their fathers because they worked seven days a week, going into the mines to work at 4 a.m., and arrived home so late at night that it made it impossible for the family to see each other. Mining was also very dangerous. Death or serious injury was a regular occurrence, and the pay was never enough to cover their expenses.

In the early years, miners didn't get paid for their "travel time." This meant that they did not get paid from the time they left home (which was miles away from the mine and they usually had to walk to work) until they arrived at the "face of the coal" inside the mine. In those days they had to pay for their explosives (powder, fuse and caps) that they used to blast the coal from the seam. Also, they paid for their mining gear plus carbide lights and carbide.

The coal companies built stores, houses, etc and sold the miners everything at inflated prices, thus keeping them in debt to them. Songs were written to expose the plight of the miners. One of the most indicting songs was by Tennessee Earnie Ford, entitled, "Sixteen Tons" with a telling line, "I load sixteen tons and what do I get, another day older and deeper in debt.... I owe my soul to the company store."

It was humiliating for the miner and their children when the mines were on "strike" and not working, because if the family needed groceries or clothes from the company store, they had to prove to the store manager that they really needed them. One winter I needed a pair of shoes. If you needed shoes the manager made you hold up your foot and show him the holes in the bottom of your shoes before he would "charge" a pair for you on your father's account. I had to do that on one occasion, and I never forgot the humiliation I felt.

I went bare foot during the summer most of my childhood and early teens. To get a pair of shoes was a great event. I can remember my grandfather measuring our feet with a string, tying a knot at intervals in the string as he measured each person's foot. When he returned with the shoes, the event was much like the wild African dogs you see on the Discovery Channel — the den dogs greeting the hunter dogs with unbelievable excitement as the hunter dogs cough up their prized catch of the day for the hungry pups. We pulled and tugged until we found the pair that fit the best.

The shoes were always one size bigger so that we could grow into them. They were called "brogans." They were rugged leather shoes that had no built in arch and were made to fit either foot so that they could be switched from foot to foot if need be

My very first pair of shoes came when I was a child about three or four years old. My parents saved up enough money (probably a dollar or two) to order me a pair of shoes from a company called The Walter Field Mail Order Company. When they came, they fit me perfectly. I felt that I could wade through a river with them and that is what I did, except, it was a small stream near our house.

I wadded up and down the little stream. Then, I began to notice that I didn't have any soles on the bottom of my shoes. All I had were the "uppers." They were made out of leather, but the soles that had gone bye, bye, were made out of cardboard paper. So much for my brand new shoes! I didn't get a spanking, but I can still hear the panic in my mother's voice as she examined my bare feet, sliding the "uppers" up and down my legs in disbelief!

The author's father worked long hard hours in the dangerous coal mines to make a living for the family. He left for work around 4 a.m. and returned after dark. Notice the water buckets in the background. They were used to carry water for cooking and drinking purposes because there was no indoor plumbing.

Mr. Goat

———⟫◆⟪———

EVERY BOY'S DREAM is to have a pony to feed, ride and care for. My dream to own a pony turned out to be more of a nightmare the day my dad came home with a goat instead of a pony.

I never blamed Dad for the mix-up. "White Lightening" got the blame for most of Dad's "mistakes" in those days. I always believed that he though he was buying a pony for me, but the whiskey blurred his vision.

"Mr. Goat," appeared to be harmless though. After all, he only stood about five hands high., but he had two HUGH ominous horns that were half of his body weight. They curved downward like a battering ram. One day, unaware that "Mr. Goat" was behind me, I discovered that a battering ram was precisely what they were when I found myself hurled through the air about six feet off the ground. Mohammed Ali could not have hit anyone any harder.

"Mr. Goat" came with a cute little green wagon with red iron wheels. The seat was just like the old western wagons in that we could sit on the seat and hold the reigns which were suppose to guide the animal. But that didn't work for "Mr. Goat," especially when a dog came running out to the road and nipped at his heels. Then, the chase was on. Sometimes we ended up in the dog's yard or under the floor of the house, or in the creek, depending upon where the dog ran to escape "Mr. Goat's" horns.

"Mr. Goat" was very mischievous. He would catch you not looking and butt you, or grab out of your hand whatever you were eating. One day he even jumped through an open window, snatched a freshly baked pone of cornbread off the table, and escaped in a flash leaving us breadless at dinner. This act of thievery got Dad's goat, and eventually resulted in a new residence for "Mr. Goat."

The worse experience I ever had while owning "Mr. Goat" was really not his fault. In fact, I have to say that he literally saved Dad's and my life that day.

As usual, Dad was drinking and he decided to go to the store which was located a couple of miles away. He asked me to harness "Mr. Goat" to the wagon. I did and climbed up on the seat, and away we went. About halfway to the store, we met a man with a truck load of peaches. Peaches were a real treat in those days, especially in the back woods of Eastern Kentucky. Dad decided to purchase two bushels of peaches and return home.

About the time we turned around to go home, a torrential rain came, and ol' Elkhorn Creek began to swell to overflowing. When we came to the "ford" (A "ford" is a shallow place in the river, making it possible to cross.) where we had to cross to the other side, the river had flooded its banks and it was impossible to return the way we came. Normally when the river flooded, traffic was diverted up and around the mountain side, but Dad was in no mood to detour through the woods, especially carrying two bushels of peaches on his back.

Therefore, when we got to the river's edge, influenced by the whiskey, Dad wadded in leading "Mr. Goat" and me perched on the seat holding the reigns in my hands as if I were in control of the situation. I had no more control over things than when the dogs chased us, nor did "Mr. Goat" in this case. Too much alcohol can cause a person to misjudge a situation sometimes to the harm of others.

We proceeded slowly into the muddy rushing water. Instantly, we were swept away into the ragging current. I was horrified as the murky monster sucked us into it's belly in one big gulp much as did the whale that swallowed Jonah in the Bible.

There was no time to think. We just clung to "Mr. Goat" who seemed calm in the midst of the storm. In it's powerful wake the current tossed us to and fro toward a brush pile which had accumulated in the curve in the river from previous floods. We grabbed for the dead driftwood and held on for dear life. We managed to hold on with the help of the current that pressed us against the debris.

The washing about caused "Mr. Goat's" harness to become entangled, and the force of the river's current against the wagon was pulling him down under the water. There was no way to escape except to cut him free from his harness, which Dad did with his pocket knife. By this time the cold water had sobered him up.

Finally, we were able to climb out of our "watery grave" to safe ground, but we lost all the peaches. I remember seeing them float down the river, bobbing up and down, a treat for somebody or something.

Later, Dad sold "Mr. Goat," and I felt sad because he had become a part of the family. I watched the new owner drive away with "Mr. Goat" pulling the little green wagon with red wheels. It had served as a lifeboat for us that day in the river. I wondered how his new owners would treat him. I hoped they would not judge him by his appearance as I had done, but that they would come to know and appreciate him, not just as a goat, but as "Mr. Goat" as I had come to know him.

I learned a wonderful lesson from "Mr. Goat" through this experience, and that is, God works in mysterious ways, for you see, I don't think a pony could have done for Dad and me what "Mr. Goat" did for us that day.

The Day I Discovered Electricity

⟫◇⟪

OFTEN A LESSON ONE LEARNS in life can come as a shock, and a shock is precisely what happened to me the day that my cousins decided it was time for me to take Electricity 101.

All I knew abut electricity was that it made light to burn, and that was good. We didn't have such gadgets as hot plates, electric razors and curling irons.

My discovery of electricity was much different from Ben Franklin's kite and key experiment. My tools of the trade were a "drop socket" hanging down from the ceiling on the front porch, and an iron "poker." I couldn't reach the socket from the floor so my cousins got me a chair to stand on and said, "if you stick this poker into the socket something wonderful will happen."

My cousins lifted me onto the chair and handed me the poker. I raised the poker and gently inserted it into the socket. I don't remember much after that except my cousins picking me up off the floor, laughing all the time. I questioned the results of the experiment, but they assured me that I had not done the procedure correctly, and if I would hold the poker in the other hand things would be entirely different.

I refused their suggestion and decided I had learned enough about electricity for one day. However, the experiment with electricity that day was not all in vain. I did learn a couple of life principles about electricity and people which I have applied in life, and they are: Don't stick a poker in a light socket unless the breaker is off, and don't listen to people who suffer from too much inbreeding.

My First Real Fish Hook

THE DAY I PURCHASED my first fish hook was like Christmas. I longed to own a real store bought one. Fishing was always a sport I enjoyed. However the accessories needed to become a "fisherman" were expensive, and I could only dream of the day when I would be able to fish with real store-bought equipment. Oh, if I could only purchase a real fish hook I would be fulfilling a childhood dream.

It has been said that "Necessity is the mother of invention:" and I find that to be true. I would improvise with whatever happened to be within my grasp. It may sound a little old-fashioned, but it worked. I used a cane pole, twine for a line, and a fish hook hand-made from a safety pin. First I would cut off the pin's head, using the eye and the sharp pointed end bent to a fishhook's shape. Then, I would thread and tie the line through the eye of the pin. But alas, I lacked a barb to hold the fish once it was caught. I learned that it might work all right if the fish happened to be small and I could jerk it to the bank in one motion. That didn't happen very often.

When I was fortunate enough to have a catch, I would proudly put it on a stringer that I had cut from a skinny branch shaped much like a chicken wishbone, with one side missing. Later, I resorted to a gig fashioned out of a table fork. "Gigging" for fish was usually done at night using a carbide light to spot the fish. Neither method was very productive. I quickly learned that a person could starve to death if he would be depending on either method to earn a living or to help keep his family in food. Therefore, my dreams of purchasing an actual fishhook continued to be my passion.

Then came the day when my parents allowed me to walk to the Shelby Gap post office by myself to buy a fish hook and mail a letter. It was about a two mile round trip down a dirt road. I was so excited it felt like Christmas even though it was summer time. I went barefoot, but I didn't mind because my feet were as tough as any shoe leather.

The post office was located in a house, and they sold a few items of merchandise on the side such as fishing supplies. My primary interest was to buy a fish hook, but Mom's main concern was that her letter got mailed. I believe that I had a nickel, three cents for a stamp and a penny for a fish hook, which left me a penny of change to take back home.

The stamp was interesting, but the fish hook was beautiful. I admired its craftsmanship for a while and then wrapped it up in a piece of brown sack paper the postmaster gave me so I wouldn't get stuck with it. Then I proceeded to stamp Mom's letter. I was in a hurry because I couldn't wait to get back home and try out my newly purchased store-bought fish hook.

I had never mailed a letter before, so the postmaster showed me how to lick the stamp and where to put it on the letter. Then he left me alone to my task of posting the letter. I began by licking the stamp to make sure it wouldn't come off.

Then, to be sure it stuck, I licked it several times more. Maybe you have heard of the Timex watch commercial on television where the watch is put through various test to prove it durability? And then the announcer says, "Timex, the watch that takes a licking and keeps on ticking?" Well, the stamp I licked didn't stand the test… it took a licking and did not keep on "sticking." I even gave it a good pounding with my fist to aid its stick ability. Finally, the postmaster heard me pounding and realized what I had done, so he put some more glue on the stamp and it finally stuck firm, and I was able to mail it.

On the way home I admired my fish hook some more. I imagined how wonderful it would be to pull in the big ones that had eluded me at my favorite fishing hole. Now, hang on to your hat because…Have you ever heard of a "chicken fish?" Well, I hadn't either until I actually caught one.

You see, the next day it rained and I couldn't go fishing so I though I would practice my fishing skills before going the next day. I decided to practice by fishing from the porch. I positioned myself in a perfect spot, baited my hook, and cast it into the yard. I was not prepared for what happened next. Out of nowhere like a flash of lightening my uncle's game fighting rooster came from under the porch floor and gulped down the baited hook. I mean he swallowed worm, hook, line and sinker. Then he took off like a jet from a runway and began to circle around and around.

Picture this, a chicken flying in circles and me holding to the fishing pole for dear life. It was like I was flying a chicken shaped kite. The chicken was squawking and flapping, and I was hollering as loud as the chicken. Everyone in the house came out to see what all the commotion was about. Several people finally retrieved my "catch of the day," but there was no way to save the chicken, so we had a very expensive chicken dinner that evening. I was scolded for my carelessness, but it was not without a slight greasy grin on the faces of a few here and there around the table.

As I look back now I can see how I learned some valuable lesson about life in all of this. First, the postage stamp incident taught me that there are some things in life that just won't stick no matter how much effort one puts into it to make it work. And I learned that too much effort to save something or someone can be counterproductive.

The most important lesson of all is in realizing that God is always nearby to help you out of any problems you may face. In this case the postmaster was a God-send and helped me achieve success in getting Mom's letter mailed.

Second, I though that store-bought fish hooks were indestructible and would last forever…. Wrong! I remember my disappointment when my hook became hung on something in the creek. The line broke and I lost it. My heart sank when I heard the snap of the fishing line and watched the hookless line slithered through the water toward me as I pulled it in.

I learned that one should not put all of his hopes in temporal things because they don't last forever, but eternal things do. I also learned if one fishes in dangerous places, he can catch something he doesn't plan on.

But there is another moral to this story and it is this. If your line breaks and you loose your fishing hook, just remember that not only are there more fish in the sea, but there are more fish hooks down at the post office to catch them with, because fish hooks are replaceable in time.

"Rag Shaking"

⋙◆⋘

"RAG SHAKING" WAS A HUMOROUS LABEL given to a monthly event held by the Missionary Alliance Church where I lived. Items such clothes, shoes and a few toys were brought to the local school playground and dumped out in piles resembling giant ant hills on the African plains. Then at a given signal, everyone made a mad dash for the merchandise. It was not unlike a scene right out of a New York Macy's Department Store sale with people running over each other in order to get there first.

It was a sight to behold with dozens of people picking up clothes and shaking them out to see the size and color. This is how the event got its name, "rag shaking." Also, I believe the "rag shaking" was the birth of the "wave" at sporting events. Visualize, if you will, a whole school yard of people waving and shaking shirts, trousers, skirts, and sweaters up and down, up and down, up and down.

The "rag shaking" day was a time when a person might find some desperately needed shoes or coats for the winter, and if lucky, a toy for a Christmas stocking. On one occasion my mother found a ceramic turkey what-not that she kept for

45

a Christmas present for me. Who said turkeys were only for Thanksgiving? I was thrilled to get it. It was all she had to give me, and I cherished it became it was given with such love.

Love was not always the theme of many "rag shakings," because things were known to get out of hand, especially when two ladies got hold of the same garment at the same time. That resulted in a tug-of-war and occasionally blows. I think the "rag shaking" was the place where the notorious Hatfield of West Virginia and the McCoy of Kentucky feud started.

Sometimes "Rag shaking's" were a lot of fun. I enjoyed searching for things to fit me — especially shoes. And it was a treat to find an occasional plastic Cracker Jack toy which was inserted in the Cracker Jack box as a prize.

I always wanted a pair of cowboy boots, and one day I found one cowboy boot at a "rag shaking." It was my size, and I searched for the other one the entire morning but to no avail. I wore the one boot around asking if anyone had seen the other matching cowboy boot, but no one had seen a boot like mine. However, I wasn't about to give up my prize boot so I decided if the price was right I would at least own one cowboy boot in my lifetime.

I was really lucky because the lady said there was no charge for just one boot, so I headed home that day walking on one bare foot and on my new found cowboy boot. I walked proudly stepping up and down, up and down on the dirt road, imaging that the other matching cowboy boot was somewhere out there on another boy's foot, and he was also wondering who was wearing his other cowboy boot that he had found at a "rag shaking."

One day at the "rag shaking" my grandmother who, by the way, was half Cherokee Indian, found a pair of blue surge pants that fit my dad perfectly. He wore them while he courted my mother. He was ashamed to keep wearing the same blue surge pants ever time he went to court my mother, so one day he gathered some walnut bark, boiled and strained it and dyed the pants a beautiful "walnut" brown. Mother never knew the difference. She though he had two pairs of pants.

It was customary at a "rag shaking" to use the school's outdoor toilet to try on clothes. One day when everyone had left after the "rag shaking" my mother found some beautiful pictures of Jesus in the ladies' toilet. Apparently a woman had brought the pictures of Jesus with her when she was going to try on some clothes, but in her rush to get back to the "rag shaking" she left the pictures of Jesus in the toilet.

The application is so obvious. Isn't this the way we do sometimes? We get carried away with the temporal things of this life and they distract us from the eternal things that should matter the most to us. We focus our attention on careers, fame and fortune rather than the weightier things in life such as God and family, and we, literally walk away as did that woman carrying nothing but the trivia of life in comparison, and leave Jesus, the eternal One, in the toilet of materialism.

Dora, Kate, and Roy Cantrell in the yard of their home on Elkhorn Creek in Kentucky. Zetta was born there. Pictured in the background is the 8-grade school with its outhouse where the picture of Jesus was left by a hurried shopper at the Rag Shaking. It was at about this age, and at this house, where Roy learned about electricity from his cousins, and was traumatized by the Sauerkraut incident, page 59.

Grandma Dora's Baptism

MY GRANDMA DORA'S BAPTISM made a profound impression on me. I had never seen anyone get baptized the way she did. They strapped her to a chair and carried her out to the near-by creek to be baptized. One preacher held the back of the chair and another one held the bottom of the chair. They leaned her backwards and on the count of three, in the name of the Father, Son and the Holy Ghost, they dunked her under the water and brought her up again.

The reason she was baptized in a chair was because she was so weak from loss of blood. Not too long before her baptism, a dentist came through and pulled several of her teeth. She bleed so much that she had to go to bed. She just kept getting weaker and weaker and then suffered a stroke. Just before this had happened, Grandma pulled me to her side and hugged and kissed me and then called for my little sister, Kate, who was just beginning to walk. She embraced and kissed her and then said, "God bless my children." These were the last words I heard her speak.

Grandma was truly saved. I was named after her son, Roy. He came home one day and found her alone in the house shouting, clapping her hands and praising God. I have always felt that the woman I saw in the vision I had when I was a little boy was my Grandma Dora. (See *Picture In The Sky*.)

I was only about three years old, but I can remember sitting by her bed and fanning her. Even though she could not speak to me, I always felt she knew that I was there with her. She never walked again and died shortly afterward. I remember how sad everyone was. Grandpa put her picture in the headstone with a little lamb statuette on top. That lamb gave me a warm feeling inside when I touched it. I didn't know what the lamb represented at the time, but I never forgot her baptism.

I don't ever remember my dad crying, not even when his mother died. The most emotion he showed was when he and Mother were walking off the hill from the cemetery after the funeral. Dad reached out and snapped a piece of grass off and moaned in grief, but he shed no tears. Mother said to Dad, "How can you stand to lose your mother?"

He replied, "If you lost your mother you would have to stand it too."

A few months after her death, Dad shared with me a very personal incident he experienced. He said that he had been drinking and came home around midnight. Everyone was in bed, and for fear of waking them he went out to the barn to sleep in the loft. It was very cold. The fodder for the animals had been harvested and put in the barn. It was stacked around the sides of the barn loft much like tin soldiers standing shoulder to shoulder.

He remembered that he awoke during the night very cold, and he thought about his mother and how if she knew he was cold she would put a warm blanket or quilt on him. As soon as he had the though, the fodder started pitching forward and covering him completely. He loved the warmth and didn't move until morning when he crawled out from under it.

Every now and then I go back to the "Cantrell Cemetery" to visit or occasionally preach a funeral and bury a person there. When I do go back there, I always visit my little brother "Junior's" grave (See *Dat's My Star*). I also visit Grandpa and Grandma's graves, and I never fail to gently caress the little lamb atop Grandma's tombstone. It gives me great comfort to reconnect with her memory.

But even more meaningful is how the little lamb on her tombstone has stuck in my mind all these years. It is the focal point of everything I remember about her. In reality, the little lamb on Grandma's headstone turned out to be symbolic of what we both share in Jesus Christ our Savior, who is the true Lamb who washes away the sins of the world. (John 1:29; Exodus 12:3; Isaiah 53:7)

Perils of a "Foot Log"

THE APPALACHIAN PLATEAU was a wonderful place to live, especially if you were a child. The mountains were full of game to hunt, and the streams were full of a variety of fish.

Some of my most pleasant memories from childhood were made around the times Dad and I went fishing in Elkhorn Creek. There was a wonderful place just below the ole' Cantrell home place in the bend of the river. We called it "The Beech Tree Hole." It always yielded up a string of fish anytime you went, that is, until the coal mining industry came in and polluted the rivers, and the dynamite poachers blasted the fish by the tubs full.

I loved it when a quick shower would come and Dad would say to me, "Roy, get us some worms and the fishing poles, and we'll go catch us a mess of fish for dinner." The showers made the water murky, and the fish couldn't see us sneak up on them. Also the rain washed bugs and worms into the stream for the fish to feed on them.

I knew the perfect place to dig the worms. It was out back of the old barn. The best bait container was a discarded Prince Albert tobacco can. Those who used tobacco either rolled their own or dipped snuff. Dad smoked Prince Albert tobacco so we had plenty of cans for worm and spare fish hooks.

The ingenuity of mountain people making something out of nothing always amazed me. For example, the ladies used tobacco cans to make hair benders to curl their hair. They would remove the ends of the tobacco cans. They would then flatten the cans with a hammer and then cut them into small strips, wrap the metal strips with strips of brown paper bags, and roll the hair on the homemade curlers that incidentally made a perfect curl.

Another use for the Prince Albert cans was to cut circular pieces from them and cover rat holes. A many a rat's purpose was thwarted by Price Albert blocking his hole. One case I heard about was a man who was wakened one night by a "thud, thud, thud" sound coming from the kitchen. When he went to investigate the noise he found that a huge rat had stolen the last piece of salt bacon in the house. He had dragged it to his hole but could not get it through it. The "thud" sound was the rat trying to pull the meat through his hole. The man wrestled the piece of meat from the rat, cut off the bit marks, washed it, and had it for breakfast the next morning.

To get to the fishing hole we had to cross Elkhorn Creek on a "foot log" which was a tree that had fallen and was placed strategically across the creek to serve as a bridge. A "foot log" could be perilous to walk on, especially if the rough bark had peeled off. Even when it was dry with the bark on it, one had to be extremely careful. If it got wet, the surface would become as slick as glass and very dangerous, especially if the river was up.

It was raining the day we went fishing, and the "foot log" was wet. We had caught several fish that afternoon and were returning home when I fell off the log. I had been the first one to arrive at the infamous "foot log" and I immediately began to cross it, placing one foot in front of the other, doing a balancing act with the worms in one hand and a string of fish in the other. Dad warned me to be careful when crossing since it was wet, but I ignored his advice to my peril. About midway across, without warning, my foot slipped and I plunged headlong into the rushing current. Over and over I tumbled while being pushed along the river with the force of a run-a-way train.

All I remember next was Dad's strong hands grabbing me and pulling me to the river's bank. He had jumped in to rescue me. When he pulled me out of the muddy water I was covered head-to-toe with sand and silt. The amazing thing was that I still had the string of fish and the worm can in my hands.

But the most amazing miracle of all was many years later when my father was drowning in a river of despair. God reversed our rolls and used me to throw him the gospel lifeline and help pull him to safety. (See *The Day Dad Got It*.) He was baptized in water and joined the church. My brothers and sisters and I preached his funeral.

To God be the glory!

Yellow Jackets

THE DAY I ATTACKED a Yellow Jacket's nest with a stick was the day I decided learning to read was an absolute necessity.

I was blessed in my family with cousins who knew a lot about most everything. At least that is what they told me. They taught me about electricity (See "The Day I Learned About Electricity".) It was a lesson I never forgot. Then there was the time the same cousins who taught me about electricity offered to teach me about how to wipe out a whole nest of yellow jackets with a stick. I had never seen a nest up close and personal until the day they took me by the hand and led me to the exact spot of the infamous yellow jacket "learning center."

We went up the old sled road which began at the mouth of Panther Branch. This was the place in the creek where I waded in my "new shoes." (See "New Shoes") The road went up the creek by Uncle Roy's house where I was born with the help of a mid-wife, my great aunt Caroline Kelley Vanover.

Immediately past the house, the road made a turn to the left and then it got very steep. It was at the place where the road went up the hill that the yellow jackets had made their nest under an old tree root that crossed the road. I didn't know it at the time but I had been led like a sheep to the slaughter. This is where literacy comes in handy. If I had been able to read I could have avoided a whole lot of pain at this moment in my life. Here is what I could have learned about yellow jackets...

"Do not use a stick to kill yellow jackets. Use a commercial wasp spray. Do this on a cool night, not during the day. If you bother them during the heat of the day, you could be in for a battle. The yellow jacket stinger is not like a regular honey bee stinger which comes out with one sting. You can receive multiple stings from one wasp because the stinger moves in and out very rapidly."

My all-knowing cousins were kind enough to give me the scoop on how to kill yellow jackets. They said "Just take this stick (the one they were so kind to provide) and beat the hole as hard and fast as you can and in doing so you will kill them as they come out of their hole."

Of course, I was told if I ran they would chase me down and really hurt me. So I beat the hole as hard and fast as I could and as long as I could stand it until I figured out that running couldn't hurt any worse than standing there swatting them.

Afterward, I had yellow jackets in my hair, in my trousers and anywhere else one could find an opening, but I really couldn't blame them for stinging. I was the one to blame for invading their space. They were just defending their family.

However, I learned a lot from the unpleasant incident that day. I learned to count to almost one hundred pointing to each one of the little red splotches on my body left from the stings. The other thing I learned was that ignorance is definitely not bliss.

Sauerkraut

⟫◆⟪

BELIEVE IT OR NOT there are some people who love sauerkraut, and I am one of them. When my dad got drunk he loved to
drink the juice of the kraut. He said it settled his stomach. What
he did one day with Mother's kraut upset all of our stomachs.

It was late summer and Mother had canned several cans
of sauerkraut. We lived in what was known as the "school house
bottom" (See photo on page 48.) This only meant that we lived
at the end of the playground of the old one-room school house.
By this time there were four children in our family: Me, Kate,
Dora and Zetta. Zetta was only a few months old. Dad's brothers, Woodrow and Caz, were drinking with Dad on this particular
day when the fight of all fights broke out over the sauerkraut.

Dad kept drinking the juice off the kraut and leaving the
kraut to ruin. Mother, who had worked very hard to can the
kraut for winter, simply made a comment that sent Dad into
orbit. She suggested that Dad pour some water in the jars that
he had drained the juice from and let it set for a while and then
drink that juice before opening another jar. Well, he took major
offense at what she said and began to carry jars of kraut out to
the front porch and pitch them into the yard, breaking the glass

fruit jars of kraut, one by one. Naturally Mother was upset and she began to cry. Of course, when she cried, all of us children began to cry. Seeing Mother cry upset my uncle Caz, and he tried to stop Dad from destroying the kraut.

Now my uncle Caz was a gentle soul. He had served in World War II and was captured by the Germans twice in North Africa. In fact, he carried my baby picture all through the war with him. He said that during his capture my picture gave him hope of getting back home. I had the privilege of winning him to Christ at the Veterans Hospital in Kingsport, Virginia and later preached his funeral. Uncle Caz never married.

When he tried to stop Dad from destroying Mother's kraut, push came to shove and the fight was on! My uncle Woodrow was there that day, and when Uncle Caz and Dad began to mix it up, Uncle Woodrow joined in the fray.

When Uncle Woodrow got drunk he wanted to go to sleep. Alcohol has different affects on people. They tell me it has to do with the way the liver digests sugar in alcohol. If the liver doesn't digest the sugar well, then, according to studies, the alcohol serves as a depressant. But if the liver digests the sugar well, then the alcohol serves as a stimulant. I always wanted Uncle Woodrow to be my father because he went to sleep when he got drunk, but Dad was just the opposite. He stayed awake forever.

When fights break out between drunks anything can happen. There was a "chop block," (a large block of wood used to chop wood on) a few yards away with an ax sticking in it. Mother told me to run and get the ax because if one of them got hold of it, someone could get seriously injured. I ran and got the ax, and on my way back to where Mother was standing, I heard her scream to watch out. Uncle Woodrow threw a huge rock at me, but I ducked just in time. We were all either crying or yelling, and "Mr. Goat" (See "Mr. Goat.") was running around trying to figure out what was going on.

Finally, Dad and my two uncles became exhausted from mostly swinging at each other and missing. They stopped and made peace, but the emotional damage was done to us children. The eye of the storm had passed, but there was more to come. The families of alcoholics always live in a state of fear of the next crises.

After Dad caught his breath, he ran Mother off and would not let her take Zetta, the baby. This left all of us children at home with Dad, including the baby who was still breast feeding, with nothing to eat.

After Mother left, Dad sent me on an errand to borrow something from his aunt Caroline, who lived a quarter mile or so down the road. I waded across the shallow part of the creek near our house. Just as I got across, I heard my mother's voice call my name.

She whispered, "Roy, don't be afraid. I am watching you and the children from here, and I plan to come and get the baby when it gets dark. I will always be watching to see that you are o.k."

I can't tell you how much her words comforted me. Her voice and presence made everything alright.

Sure enough, that night Mother came and got Zetta while we were asleep. She knew that when Dad sobered up he would be different, but in the meantime we had to ride out the storm. I can remember having only watermelon to eat, but we survived, even "Mr. Goat" who ate the melon rind.

As always, when things got back to "normal", as normal as could be, Dad was remorseful for what he had done, but it was too late because the emotional scars were already imprinted on our young brains. We would carry them for the rest of our lives. The bright side is that we had a mother who was the super glue of the family, and she was there to comfort us.

There is no voice sweeter than a mother's voice. Shortly after Dad burned my school books ("A Fire That Won't Go Out"), and I had to go back to Grandmother's house to live and go to high school, Mother came to check on me. We were all in bed when she arrived. I heard her call my name from the road.

The reason I heard my mother's voice was because I knew her voice. I read a story some years ago about then fire chief Bonner of New York, who said that he had an alarm installed in his house that sounded when there was a fire in the city. The irony is that his wife never heard it go off. On the other hand, he said that if the baby cried in the next room, his wife could hear it, but the baby's cry never woke him. Mother's voice roused me.

My cousin (who is now Dr. Ira B. Potter, practicing medicine in Lackey, Kentucky) who is more like a brother to me than a cousin, said, "I didn't hear anything."

Then my mother called again. I jumped out of bed and ran outside to meet her. A car had dropped her off beside the road across the traintrack from the house. I was elated to see her.

There is one voice, however, that is sweeter than all the other voices, including a mother's. It is the voice of Jesus who said "My sheep know my voice and a stranger they will not follow."

I heard the sweet voice of my Lord and Savior Jesus Christ call my name and ask me to open the door of my heart to Him. I did May 20, 1958, and His voice has been with me in daily communication ever since.

The beautiful old Hymn, *In The Garden* says it best: "And He walks with me, and He talks with me, and He tell me that I am His own, and the joy we share as we tarry there none other has ever known." This beats sauerkraut all to pieces!

Broken Arm

⟨⟩◆⟨⟩

THE DAY I BROKE MY ARM was the worse physical pain I had ever experienced. It was a freak accident. Kate, my oldest sister, and I were playing at the old log barn next to our log house. Both were built by Dad and his brother just a few yards from Grandpa's board and batten house. Our house and the barn had rived white oak single roofs.

The front of the barn was made with an overhang in front so that the horse could pull the sled loaded with fodder or hay under it to shelter from the rain. The hay could be unloaded and lifted up through the ceiling made out of poles and stored back in the barn. I climbed up onto the poles of the overhang, and Kate was tickling my feet with a corn stalk. My foot slipped, and I fell between the poles onto the ground. I hit my right arm on a rock and broke it one inch above the elbow.

My parents took me to Grandpa's house next door so he could examine my arm to see if it was broken. He said that it was broken, and he suggested that a splint be made to hold my arm in place, but mother insisted that it needed to be professionally set by a doctor.

Mother and I made our way out of the holler with me holding my arms close to my chest. The pain was excruciating.

I cried each time I took a step. Mother carried me to lessen the pain. As I envision this love of hers in carrying me to the doctor, it reminds me of Mary Stevenson's poem, "Footprints in the Sand."

Thank God that Mother insisted on taking me to the doctor, because the doctor said that if my arm had not been properly set by him, my upper arm between my elbow and shoulder would not have developed.

The cast came off in about six weeks, and I was no worse for the wear. All my family and friends signed it, and I kept it for a while as a trophy. Even thought all the evidence of a broken arm soon vanished, I never forgot the love and compassion and wisdom of my mother. If it had not been for her I would have a crippled arm today.

My mother's compassion for me reminds me of God's love. No matter how badly we mess up, God loves us and will take us in his arms and bind up our wounds and heal or hurts. King David said when others forsake us then the Lord will take us up. (Psalm 27:10)

It reminds me of the beautiful Scripture that says "A bruised reed He will not break, and a smoldering (dimly burning) wick He will not quench, till He brings justice and a just cause to victory." (Matthew 12:20)

Four Pound Lard Bucket

BACK IN THE TIME when people used lard instead of Crisco, lard came in metal containers in various sizes. My favorite was the 4lb. bucket. It was the perfect size to carry my lunch to school. Mother filled it with whatever was left over from dinner the night before - such things as green beans and cornbread and maybe an onion. Sometimes it was filled with pinto beans that we called soup beans and cornbread. But my favorite was sweet milk (We called buttermilk 'sour milk.') and cornbread. Oh, did I tell you the bucket had equal markings on the side to remind us how much we could eat, because I had to share the contents with the other siblings?

That old 4lb. lard bucket was extremely durable. We had to walk to school down a railroad track. One day the cuff of my trousers hung on a railroad spike, and I fell extending my "lunch bucket" forward and down onto a cross tie. I bent it almost in half, but the lid did not come off and my lunch was saved. I stared at its versatility in amazement.

The old school I attended was featured on the front cover of *Life Magazine* one year, along with a story reporting the poverty stricken area of Eastern, Kentucky. I can remember going to school with holes in the seat of my pants and wearing no underwear. I walked sideways so that the other students couldn't see me and make fun. I don't know which was worse, wearing trousers with holes in them, or wearing Grandpa's old wool pants cut off where the crotch dragged the ground. Wearing them was like wearing pants made out of steel wool.

The story is told about a little girl who was taken to a local hospital suffering from malnutrition. When the nurses saw her condition they quickly brought her a glass of milk. They noticed later that she wasn't drinking any of it, and they knew she had to be hungry. The nurses asked the little girl why she wasn't drinking her milk. Her reply was, "How far down can I drink?" Her answer reflected the poverty in her home where several children had to share a glass of milk. Our situation was similar when we were growing up. We shared everything at home, and especially our lunch at school which we ate from a 4lb lard bucket.

Since I was he oldest child, I was in charge of distributing the food from the bucket. When the teacher rang the bell for dinner we all scrambled for the best place to eat. If it was summer time we usually ate outside under the school house or found a place under a tree or sat on rocks. There was no grass because we usually beat it down playing games. All of the school children gathered in little family groups to share their lunch. If they were fortunate enough, some students lived close to their houses and could go home to eat. That is, if they had anything to eat at all.

Usually when dinner time came, my sisters wanted to play, so I let them eat first. Mother always put a spoon in the bucket for us to share. It was difficult to spoon the cornbread from the bottom of the bucket so, anxious to play, my sisters would turn the bucket up and drink the milk leaving most of the cornbread in the bottom of the bucket.

We always kept a sharp eye on the marks on the side of the bucket to make sure no one got more than their share. However, I learned a great lesson about milk and cornbread when I shared lunch with my sisters. That is cornbread always sinks to the bottom, and if one is patient and waits to be the last one to eat, he gets the most. This principle applies in everyday life, because the best in life comes to those who wait. Patience has its virtues.

"Blessed are they who hunger and thirst after righteousness for they shall be filled." (Matthew 5:6)

Roy Cantrell, kneeling second from left in second row, is pictured with all the other students in his 8 grade school. None of his siblings are pictured in this photograph. At right is the outhouse where the picture of Jesus was left by a hurried shopper at the Rag Shaking.

Wipeout!

—⟫◈⟪—

THE FIRST TIME I EVER REMEMBER wanting my dad to get back what he dished out was when he spanked my infant sister Zetta. She was crying like all babies do when they are wet or hungry. He was drunk as usual, and her crying irritated him. He spanked her over and over again which caused her to cry even more. Mother and I begged Dad not to whip her, but he wouldn't listen, so she finally took the baby from him and left for her sister's house until he sobered up.

The next day Dad found out where Mother was staying, so he took me with him to beg her to come back home. He flagged down a big coal dump truck and asked them to give us a ride. The cab was full, so the driver lifted me up into the back of the truck, and Dad rode on the running board. In the truck bed with me were two huge steel mining car wheels and axles that weighed hundreds of pounds each. I was told to stand up and hold on to the rear window frame. Those instructions saved my life.

Dad and the people inside the truck were talking, and the driver was about to pass the place where dad wanted to get off, so he yelled "Stop!" When Dad yelled, the driver threw on his air brakes, and we came to a screeching halt. The sudden stop threw Dad off the running board of the truck in the nearby bushes, but no one saw where he landed.

In the meantime, the steel wheel and axles in the truck bed rolled forward and slammed against the cab with such a tremendous force that they would have killed me or crippled me for life, except for the fact that the wheels hit first. This left a space between the truck cab and the axle where I was standing.

Everyone was looking for Dad but we couldn't find him. It was as if he had vanished from the face of the earth. Then, a faint sound was heard coming from the nearby culvert. It was Dad, he had been thrown into the culvert where a growth of trees covered it, and the bushes cushioned his fall. Except for a few cuts and bruises he was okay. There is an old saying in the mountains of eastern Kentucky that God watches over fools and drunks, or was that preachers and drunks?

The truck drivers pulled Dad out of the culvert and took him up the branch to my aunt Bess's house where Mother was staying. Mother nursed him back to health, and eventually she went back home with him. I don't recall him whipping Zetta for no reason again. What happened is in the past now, but at the time I felt that Dad got what he deserved for whipping my baby sister.

I found it difficult to close this story on a positive note, but then I remembered a story I read of a man who dreamed that he saw Jesus tied to a post and a man beating Jesus with a whip. The scene could have been taken from the *Passion of the Christ* movie by Mel Gibson. The man dreaming said that he was so angry at the person beating Jesus that he wanted to inflict the same pain on him, but all he could do was beg him to stop. At some point in the dream the man with the whip turned around, and to the amazement of the man who was dreaming, it was he himself who was beating Jesus!

There is no excuse for Dad's abuse, but his sin should remind us that we, "All have sinned and come short of the glory of God." (Romans 3:23)

Yes, that is why we are bound to forgive those who trespass against us, because when you really think about it…. IT IS A WIPEOUT!

Don't Tell

—◆—

THE "BLUE AND WHITE" was a whiskey store where Dad hung out when he was drinking. It was not a nice place for a child, but Dad took me there unbeknownst to Mother, not that she would have had any say in the matter. For some unknown reason, Dad did not want Mother to know that we had visited the place, so he bought me a whole carton of Kool-Aid and told me not to tell her where we had been. I eagerly agreed to the deal.

I had never seen so much Kool-Aid at one time. There was a rainbow of colors in the carton: grape, orange, strawberry and lime. I felt like I was the luckiest boy in the whole wide world.

Dad and I walked home that night without a flashlight. He was staggering from side to side and clinging to me. I could barely hold him up. It was scary, especially when he wanted to walk the white line in the middle of the road, even when cars were coming. I watched for the headlights of the cars and warned Dad, but he would not get out of the road, so the cars went around us. I was so glad we finally make it home alive.

When we arrived home, I immediately went to Mother and showed her my carton of Kool-Aid. She didn't know that I wasn't supposed to tell her where it came from; therefore, she naturally wanted to know where I got so much Kool-Aid.

I blurted out ,"Dad bought it for me at the "Blue and White." Whoops! Big mistake!

Dad got very angry at me for telling Mother where we had been that night. To punish me, he made me give him all of the Kool-Aid and bring him a half gallon jar of water. I did what he said, and he began to open the packages of Kool-Aid and pour them into the jar. I began to cry because I though he was going to make me drink the mixture without any sugar.

When he told me that I didn't have to drink the jar of Kool-Aid. I was relieved. But I never forgot the incident. Even to this day I can still see that awful dirty mixture of Kool-Aid in the fruit jar. The repulsive mixture represented the confusion in my little heart. Instantly all the beautiful colors in my spirit were turned into a dreadful grey and the "don't tell" rule was indelibly stamped on my memory forever.

My mother's face was filled with pain for me as she helplessly watched Dad poured my packages of Kool-Aid into the fruit jar. I wanted to comfort her and say, "Don't worry, Mother. I won't remember all of this when I grow up, and I won't tell anyone." But I did!

Aunt Mae's Magical Door

DOORS COME IN ALL SHAPES, sizes and colors. They serve various purposes, but they all have one thing in common. They open and shut – all of them except Aunt Mae's magical door.

Aunt Mae lived in the mouth of Big Branch in a board and batten house. The walls inside were made of plain one-inch rough lumber, so it was easy to make a new doorway by sawing out a hole in the wall. To get to Aunt Mae's house we had to walk from the main road about two miles uphill, stepping on rocks most of the way to avoid walking in water because the road was in the middle of the stream.

Now imagine this... five or six children getting off the school bus at the mouth of the branch, already tired after going to school and riding on the bus for two hours that day, and then having to hike over two miles uphill with a load of book to boot. By the time they arrive home they were hungry and exhausted.

I occasionally spent the night with my cousins, and I remember how difficult it was to trudge up the holler to Aunt Mae's house. The treck was not a lot of fun except for the time when Aunt Mae pulled her magic door trick and we all howled.

Picture this scene. A half dozen children strung out down the holler making their way to the house, famished, occasionally dropping a book or two, and usually fussing about something. Finally they arrive at the house, and they enter through the kitchen door.

Now here is where things take a turn… Before this we would pass from the kitchen into the next room which was located straight ahead, where we deposited the school books on the bed and headed for the dining table to eat. The bedroom "door" was an old army blanket that Aunt Mae tacked up over the doorway for privacy. That is until Aunt Mae decided to close up the door that day and make another entrance from another room into that bedroom. But she didn't stop there; she decided to tack the army blanket back over the now boarded up doorway and wait for the children to arrive

My cousin and I arrived first. It is amazing how the smell of food can energize a person when he is really hungry. James lowered his head like a bull charging a matador, struck the wall covered with the army blanket with full force, and bounced back into a spread eagle position on the floor with books everywhere. Dazed, but no worst for wear, he got up scratching his head and staring at the army blanket in amazement as if to say, "How did I miss the door that much?"

Aunt Mae, who was watching with glee, explained what she had done, but asked us to be quiet and wait for the others.

Sure enough, one by one, each child repeated what the last one had done. Then the previous victims jumped up and down with laughter as each person hit the wall and fell backwards onto the floor. This may seem cruel, but it was so funny. No one was hurt, except maybe for a few bruised egos. I will never forget Aunt Mae's magical door trick because it brought a lot of laughter to us, which was rare in those days. I'm sure Aunt Mae never did either and wore the story out telling it over and over again.

Aunt Mae's magical door was a false one and non-accessible, but God has a magical door that opens into life eternal and that is always accessible to whosoever will enter. That door is Jesus Christ! (Read John 10:7-9.)

NEW RIVER AND POCAHONTAS CONSOLIDATED COAL CO.

BERWIND, W. VA., _____ No. 24

IN ACCOUNT WITH *James Cantrell*

Period From _____ to OCT 15 1950 19____

CREDITS			OTHER DEBITS		
Days at			New River & Poca. Stores	3	99
Days at			Federal Social Sec. Tax	1	69
Hours at.			Check Weighman		55
			Fed. Income Tax		
Correction			Retirement Fund		
66 Tons at	46	66	Savings Bonds		
13 at	10	30	Suggestee Executions		
at			Rent	4	15
9 Yards at 64	14	72			
at			Water		
2nd and 3rd Shift	2	74	Coal	5	40
Increase at	33	25	Hauling	1	48
O. T. & T. T.	7	96	Doctor	3	-
Mine Checks			Hospital	3	80
TOTAL CREDITS	115	13	Insurance	3	-
			Cash Advanced		
Occupational Deductions			Overdraft		
Explosives	2	50	Corrections		
Con. Sales Tax	0	7	Burial Fund	1	50
Mine Checks			Consumer's Sales Tax		
			Union Dues	4	-
TOTAL DEDUCTIONS	2	57	Initiation Fee		
			Land Leases		
TAXABLE EARNINGS	112	56	Bus		
Cash Held			Telephone		
			Bath House		
E. & O. E. Total			Total	112	56
Overdraft			Balance Due		

RETAIN THIS STATEMENT

Dad's two-week pay receipt. Notice that expenses exactly equal receipts.

The Rattlesnake

ALCOHOL CAN INFLUENCE A PERSON to do things that they would never do when they are sober.

My Dad worked in the coal mines of eastern Kentucky and West Virginia all of his adult life. In fact, he died from a miner's disease called "black lung" which clogs the lungs with coal and rock dust and makes it hard and then impossible to breathe. There are three stages to the disease. The third stage was the worst case and resulted in death usually within six months. Growing up in the coal fields I saw many miners suffer from this plight. In my dad's younger days, before he got "black lung," he would climb the Appalachian Mountains without any problem, especially if he had a little whiskey in him.

I never understood why Dad drank so much until I was older. Then I realized that part of his addiction was to dull the fear of facing death in the mines every day. The mine was a death trap. He watched his buddies get crushed to death and saw their families suffer. It was a war zone he went through every day. One enemy was a silent killer that lurked overhead. A "kettle bottom" could drop suddenly and kill a person without warning. A "kettle bottom" is a rock formation in the ceiling of the mine that is round on the top and flat on the bottom. The boulder gets its name from its kettle shape. Though it appears to be part of a solid roof, the danger occurs when the coal is removed from under the "kettle bottom." With no support under it, it can fall without warning onto its unsuspecting victim.

Furthermore, the reason "kettle bottoms" are so deadly, is that they appear solid when the miner tests them using his "coal pick" (a tool with two pointed ends used to dig coal). Normally, if the mine roof is safe, it sounds solid when the miner hits it with his pick. When he hits a "kettle bottom" it sounds as solid as the rest of the roof, even to the most experienced miner.

If a person is intoxicated while working in the mines the danger of getting killed is even worse. In fact, intoxication is and was the cause of many a person's death in the mines. Dad drank a lot, but I never knew him to go into the mines drunk.

However, I do remember one time when alcohol almost caused my father's death. He was very drunk this particular day when he decided to climb a fire tower on top of a nearby mountain. He insisted that I, along with my two sisters Kate and Dora, accompany him. We were excited about the adventure until the return trip when a rattlesnake changed everything.

We packed a lunch and set out on our adventure. After several hours we reached the vacant fire tower and managed to climb part way up. We returned to the ground safe but exhausted. The trip back was going well until the girls who had lagged behind came upon a huge mountain rattlesnake.

"There's a big snake, and it is trying to bit us," they screamed. I ran to them as fast as I could, and sure enough there was one of the biggest rattlesnakes I had ever seen, coiled and ready to strike.

I was about to kill the snake when Dad stopped me. He wanted to capture it. We begged him to let us kill the snake or let it go, but he insisted on taking it with us. He made me cut a forked stick and bring it to him. I did, and he placed the fork of the stick over the snake's head and held it firmly against the ground. He had me remove one of my shoe strings, and he tied the snake's head to the stick. We knew capturing the snake spelled trouble, and we were right.

When we arrived back home later that evening we put the snake in a large glass jar and punched holes in the lid so that the snake could breathe. We poked fun at the snake by tapping on the glass and jumping backwards when he would strike at us. This went on for a while until Dad decided to prove to us that those religious people down the road were not the only ones who could handle snakes. Sometimes religion and alcohol can cause a person to do some strange things.

The drama took place on our small back porch which was covered with a linoleum rug. Dad sat down on the linoleum and demanded that the snake be brought to him so that he could show us how to "handle" a snake just like some of the church people he had heard about. He promised us there was nothing to it. We were all scared stiff, and religion or no religion, we didn't want to be near a snake - let alone handle one.

He removed the lid while giving us a lecture from his imaginary book on "How to Handle Snakes for Dummies." He took the lid off the jar and dumped the snake out onto the floor. It landed between his spread legs with a thud and immediately coiled up into a striking position. Still Dad paid no attention to the snake but continued to lecture us on the art of snake handling. I think the snake was as confused and frightened as we were.

During the pause, the rattlesnake decided to run for cover, but the linoleum was too slippery, and he just slid from side to side as if he was crawling on sand. We yelled that he was getting away. Dad reached and snatched the snake by the tail and pulled him back between his legs. Again the snake assumed a striking position.

The snake tried to escape several times. Each time Dad would pull it back by its tail, pick it up by its head, and put it back on the floor. After he finished his demo on how to handle a snake, he decided that it was time for his "students" to practice what he had taught. We children turned to Mother with eyes pleading for help.

She was a godly Christian and had been praying all the time for God's to intervene, and He did. She began to pray aloud for God to protect Dad and her children from harm. There was a peace that came over the place, and Dad picked up the rattlesnake and put it back into the jar. Then he took it out in the yard and killed it.

Later when Dad sobered up, Mother told him what had happed the day before. (Most of the time he never knew what he did when he was drunk.) She told him how he could have been bitten and killed, or how one of the children could have died. It really shook him up. She explained how her prayer had protected all of us from serious injury or death.

Even though my dad was not a religious man, this incident made an impact on his life. I know it did for all of us children. We never forgot how God delivered us from the fangs of the rattlesnake that day. But also we knew that He had saved us from an even more formable serpent – that old serpent, the Devil. It was all through the prayers of our godly mother.

Quarantined!

—◆—

LIKE A DEADLY TSUNAMI hitting a peacefully sleeping village, the news came that Novella, our 14 month old baby sister had contracted polio. The first shock wave came in the form of an eerie red sign with bold black letters. It read "Quarantined!" We watched in horror as the mining company doctor nailed the ominous sign to the exterior of our house. He gave us a stern warning not to leave the premise or allow anyone to enter upon penalty of prosecution. The only exception to the quarantine was that Dad could go to work in the coal mines and come straight back home.

It is amazing how much psychological damage a child can suffer from an 11 X 14 size cardboard sign with the word "Quarantined" written on it. Even after the sign was removed, it took months just to feel normal again. Even to this day, I can sense the isolation and humiliation I felt back then. It was no one's fault, but the experience was devastating.

Dr. Emory E. Lovus was the company doctor who examined Novella. He told Mother, "She has a little paralysis, and we need to send her to the hospital in Welch, West Virginia (the county seat of McDowell County) for further tests."

The doctors at the hospital in Welch confirmed that she had polio and recommended that she be transferred to the Milton Memorial Hospital in Milton, West Virginia. When Novella was hospitalized she had paralysis only in her right arm, but the disease progressed, and we were notified that she had paralysis all over her body and had to be put in an "iron lung."

An iron lung was a respirator used on polio suffers with chest paralysis. The machine was almost the length of a subcompact car. It exerted a push-pull motion on the chest. It made a noise like "whoosh, whoosh, whoosh," and it was so noisy that you could only speak between "whooshes."

Polio paralyzed its victims by killing off the spinal cord's motor-nerve cells that control various muscles. In the case of respiratory paralysis, the chest loses its muscle action, and the patients are in danger of suffocation because they cannot get enough air into their lungs.

Thousands were afflicted with the polio virus before a vaccine was developed by Dr. Jonas Salk in 1955. The polio virus lives in dirt and water and is transmitted from feces. When it enters the stomach, it attacks cells in the central nervous system which control muscle functions. The reality for a polio patient was that the iron lung would latterly squeeze the chest to expand and contract the rib cage so they could breathe.

Since the disease was contagious, we were all quarantined. The company store, which housed the little post office and grocery store, charged food on Dad's account and sent food and mail to us. We watched the delivery people through the window as they hurriedly came and dropped off items on the front porch and then left as quickly as they came. It was as if they were avoiding the leprosy.

We all suffered from the quarantine, even our friends, but Novella was the real victim. She was taken from her family at the age of 14 months old and put in an "iron lung" for 29 days. A lot of prayers were said for Novella's health.

Then the second shock wave of the tsunami came two weeks into Novella's tragedy. Junior, the sibling next to her, who was three and a half years old at the time she got sick, choked on a piece of coconut cake and died. To further complicate matters, Mother was 6 months pregnant with her 7th child, Auldin. She almost last him due to the trauma.

However, in spite of it all God was faithful! After much prayer, Mother said that God assured her Novella would be paralyzed in her right arm, but that she would be able to walk. She had not taken one step before she was stricken with polio, but walk she did. The next report from the hospital informed us that they were bringing her home and that we could pick her up at the local company store.

Even though the death of Junior caused the family great consternation, the good news from the hospital about Novella's recovery lifted our spirits and was cause for rejoicing. Also, three months later Auldin was born. He was almost a clone of Junior. Auldin's birth was a gift from God, and his birth couldn't have come at a better time.

Finally the quarantine was lifted and we went back to life as usual. Even though the trauma we suffered had taken its toll on us psychologically, in other ways we were better for the experience. We became a closer knit family and expressed our love for one another even more. We were also richer spiritually.

During the time we were quarantined we drew strength from the Bible because it contained many examples of people who were "quarantined" for one reason or another but came through it better than before. Such people were:

- Noah and his family were in the ark for almost a year.
- Moses was isolated on the back side of the desert.
- David along with 600 men fled from king Saul and lived in the cave of Adullum for months.
- Joseph was falsely accused and imprisoned for years.
- Daniel was put in prison and then cast into the lion's den.
- The three Hebrew children were imprisoned and cast into a fiery furnace.
- Jesus spent 40 days in the wilderness tempted by Satan.
- Paul was imprisoned in Rome for over a year, not to mention the time he spent alone in Arabia after his conversion.
- John the Beloved was exiled to the Isle of Patmos where he wrote the book of Revelation.

Novella is an adult now and I called her to get her reflections on what had happened to her. She told me her story. She said that she can vaguely remember the hospital stay in Milton. She remembers nothing about the iron lung. She only remembers walking down a path with some nurses to where several other medical people were looking at her through a black iron fence. Her memory is that the iron bars made her feel caged like an animal.

She said that when she started school there were questions in her mind about why she was crippled. One day she asked Mother why she got polio and why none of the other children got it. She recalled that Mother posed a question.

She asked, "Novella, if you could give your crippled arm to one of your siblings right now, which one would you give it to?"

Her answer was, "I wouldn't give it to either one of them because they couldn't stand it." Her answer revealed the pain that she had gone through. She didn't wish it visited on anyone else in the family.

I asked her to tell me how the crippled arm had affected her in life. She told me about the time she wanted to mop the floor when she was a little girl and Mother told her that she couldn't do it because she couldn't wring out the mop dry enough with one hand. She kept pleading with Mother to let her mop the floor. While the debate was going on between them, Dad had been listening.

He came to Novella's aid and said, "Let her try it. If she can't wring out the mop, you can dry the floor later."

She told me how she put the mop handle between her legs, wrapped her ankles around the mop handle and squeezed the water out of the mop with one hand. She did an admirable job moping and drying the floor that day, and that gave her more confidence to try other things.

When Novella was in her teens, she was given the opportunity to go to Chicago, Illinois to have surgery on her dislocated shoulder. The doctors wanted to fuse her arm to her shoulder which would give her more mobility and strength to lift things.

All the time she was growing up, Novella questioned why everyone in her entire community was polio free except her. Then when she went to Chicago for surgery. She explained to me that the event was like what Oprah Winfrey calls a "light bulb moment." Her "light bulb" came on when she was admitted to the hospital along with 27 other young people who needed some type of corrective surgery. She noticed that all of them were in wheelchairs. Not one of them could walk.

When she saw how blessed she was to be able to walk, she ran errands for the other patients – mostly carrying food and drinks to them. It was at that moment she thanked God for answering Mother's prayers, and it was then that she began to appreciate her ability to walk. She stopped feeling sorry for herself for having a paralyzed arm. Her experience was much like the man who said, "I complained that I had no shoes until I saw a man who had no feet."

Another "light bulb moment" for her came when she went back to the doctor after the surgery for a follow up visit. The doctor told her that of his 600 polio patients, she was the only one who did not have a curved spine. Again this verified that her ability to walk was an answer to prayer.

I asked if she saw any "blessings" in her being physically challenged.

Her answer was, "They are too numerous to tell. The thing that appeared to be my weakness has become my strength because you are only crippled if you think you are. The fact that I can walk is always a reminder of God's mercy to me. Yes, I have wondered what it would be like to toss a child into the air with both arms, or reach up in the cabinet with one hand and take down a dish. But those things that I can't do pale in comparison to what I can do. And furthermore, I believe my experience has changed my life. It has drawn me closer to God."

I listened to her give praise to God for her paralyzed arm and say how she wouldn't reverse the situation even if she could. I though about Jacob in the Bible whose name in the beginning meant "Surplanter" and "Deceiver." Then he wrestled with an angel at Bethel, and God actually struck Jacob on the thigh. That caused an injury to his leg that resulted in his using a stick to walk the rest of his life. In the process God changed Jacobs name from "Surplanter" and "Deceiver" to "Prince of God." He became the father of the nation of Israel. That injury was Jacob's "light bulb moment" in life.

The English definition of Novella is, "A novella consists of stories mid-way in terms of length and complexity, between a short story and a novel, focusing on a single chain of events with a surprising turning point. A novella is a short prose fiction derived from the Italian word for new." The Latin root is *nova* or *novia*. A novia is a type of star that decreases and increases in brightness with the passage of time.

To me all these definitions describe our Novella, because her surprising turning point was when she walked out of the hospital when she was told she would never walk again. The definition I like the most is the *novia* that is a type of star that increases with brightness, because when God chose to gift our family with Novella, He graced not only our family but the entire human race with a special star that increases with brightness and beauty with every passing day.

Sister Novella was stricken with Polio when she was still an infant, but she recovered enough to be able to walk, unlike most other victims. She is pictured in front of the Potter home place in Shelby, Kentucky. Notice the road on the other side of the railroad tracks. It was from the road that Roy's mother called to him one night. See page 62 for the story.

"Dat's My Star!"

THE WORST DAY OF MY LIFE came without warning on a mild November day in 1951. It was Sunday and we had finished a delicious meal of fried chicken and homemade coconut cake for dessert.

Our family was under quarantine because my sister had contracted polio, and she was in the hospital in an iron lung. (See "Quarantined") We were forbidden to mix socially with people. So to get out of the house, Dad and I headed for the hills right after dinner. We took the chicken entrails for bait to set our traps for a 'possum. We were barely 200 feet from the house when Kate, my oldest sister, screamed to the top of her voice. We could tell by the desperation in her cry that something terrible was wrong.

Dad dropped everything and ran down the little winding dirt path, slipping occasionally on the recently fallen leaves. He rushed toward the house and onto the little back porch. In the meantime I could see Mother in the front yard with a bundle in her arms that I learned later was "Junior," my three and a half year old baby brother. By this time neighbors gathered from every direction, ignoring the quarantine that we were under.

A couple of men took Junior out of Mother's arms. Dad arrived immediately after that, and he and the two men got in a car and raced off down Second Bottom toward the main road. The coal company provided a doctor's office in the community where we lived, but it was Sunday, and the hospital was several miles away. Sometimes the nearest doctor's office was closed because one doctor would split his hours between coal camps.

I watched the drama unfold from my vantage point on the hillside where I was still frozen in place. I had dropped to my knees when I heard Kate scream. It was as though I was watching a tragic movie play out before my eyes.

I watched the car make the sharp "U" turn at the end of the coal camp as it turned back toward me. It passed a few feet above and behind me onto a paved highway, and headed for the doctor's office in the next community.

I sat motionless on the ground for a long time, afraid to go home and face the bad news. I didn't want to know what had happened. Gradually I made my way down the hill to the house where I learned that Junior had been playing on the bed, bouncing up and down, when he regurgitated some coconut cake and choked on it.

He died in the car on the way to the hospital. I had been thrilled when Junior was born, because I had grown tired of playing house with my three younger sisters, Kate, Dora and Zetta. They were wonderful sisters, but I longed for a brother to play with. Then Junior finally came along.

When he got old enough to sleep away from Mother and Dad, he slept with me. We would lie in bed at night and talk about the events of the day and make plans for the next one. One night while we were lying in bed talking, Junior pulled on my T-shirt sleeve and pointed to a bright star just outside of our window and said to me, "Woy, dat's my star." Night after night when the sky was clear and "his star," was visible, he would say the same things to me, "Woy, dat's my star."

I did not realize how much his statement would mean to me until after his death. The first night after his funeral, I was lying in bed sobbing with tears running down my face. I was devastated by his death until I saw the star that night that he had pointed to a hundred times before he died. Yes, there in the heavens was "his star" twinkling with even more brilliance than any time before. I could hear his sweet little innocent voice say with confidence, "Woy, dat's my star."

I'm an old man now, and I still have the bed Junior and I slept in when he pointed at the "evening star" and claimed it as his own. I cannot count the times I have looked toward heaven for Junior's star since he died. I look not in a sad way, but in a joyful way, because I know he is with the Lord Jesus in heaven.

The best view I ever had of "his star" was on a night flight from Minneapolis, Minnesota to Nashville, Tennessee. I was returning from a funeral that I had preached for a dear saint of God. I was seated at a window over the wing of the plane. The sky was pitch black, and the stars we flickering like a billions fireflies on a summer night. I began to look for Junior's star. It was no where to be seen. Then, suddenly, it appeared as the plane banked a little to the right, dropping the wing for a grand view of "Junior's star."

It seemed as though no time had passed from the first time I heard him say, "Woy, dat's my star." Junior was right because the Bible says that those who die in Christ "shall shine as the firmaments of the heavens." (Daniel 12:3) I know that when I die my star will be somewhere near his, but it won't be as bright.

Junior is pictured in the center of this group. The Cantrell children were all dressed to go on vacation. Pictured, left to right, are: Roy, a Ledford boy kneeling behind his little brother, Dora, "Nookie" Cornett, Junior, Kate, Jennifer Cornett, Zetta, "Wickie" Cornett (kneeling), and another Ledford boy. They are in the Cornett's front yard in Second Bottom (Newhall), West Virginia. In the background to the right is the Cantrell home .

Moonshine Into Water

⟫◆⟪

THE FIRST TIME I EVER SAW a *bona fide* miracle was the day Mother prayed for God to turn Dad's moonshine into water. I remember the occasion very well.

It was a cold snowy Saturday in November. Dad drank a lot and when he did, things got pretty rough around the house. On this occasion he had been drinking for several days and was desperate for more. When he got in this shape he would drink anything that even had a hint of alcohol in it. I have seen him drink Mennen shaving lotion mixed with water. He was a full blown alcoholic, and it was not a pretty sight when he got drunk. Mother knew if Dad got more whiskey, it meant more trouble for the family.

Moonshine was plentiful where we lived, so it was not difficult to get it anytime. It was an unwritten code of the mountains that when a moonshiner ran off a "batch," he usually hid a half gallon or quart near the still to get later when he was running short. As a teenager I knew this code, and when I found a still, I would search for the cache. And to such a cache, Dad was headed.

We all knew when Dad got drunk that it meant he would miss work and could possibly lose his job. But, he would sell anything valuable or pawn something just for a pint of whiskey. The object pawned was very seldom redeemed. For sure, trouble in some form — lose of sleep, cursing, and often physical and mental abuse — was bound to happen.

Mom's prayers went into high gear as she prayed, "Lord, I've not been a Christian very long, but I read in your Bible that one time you turned the water into wine at the marriage of Canaan. If you are that powerful, I'm asking you to turn that moonshine that Allen is going after into water, because you know how bad he is when he drinks."

Her first cousin, Crit Vanover, was there then, and neither he nor Dad heard Mom's prayer, but I did. She was asking for a miracle. I never heard her pray with such desperation. I can still hear her words in my mind today.

I didn't know much about God, but Mother would read the stories from the Bible about Jonah and the whale, Daniel in the Lion's Den, Moses and the parting of the Red Sea, and the three Hebrew Children in the fiery furnace. I loved the stories but thought that only happened to people in the Bible stories, especially since they were referred to as "God's children." They were probably related to Him, but we weren't any kin to God. We didn't know anybody important. But Mother believed God for a miracle that day. I couldn't wait to see if the moonshine would turn to water, just as she had asked.

Dad was relentless in his pursuit, and he was going to find his hidden "cache." We (Dad, Crit, and me) arrived at the hiding spot. Dad and Crit were anxious to get their "fix." Crit uncovered a half-gallon fruit jar, opened it and handed it to Dad. He took a big drink, and spit it out immediately. He began cursing and swearing and said that it was nothing "but water." Their minds had been set on 100 proof moonshine, and the liquor turned out to be pure water!

All the way home they conversed on the fact that someone had stolen their moonshine and put water into the container. They threatened to kill the person who did it. I didn't dare tell them what Mother had prayed, but I couldn't wait for her to hear how her prayer had been answered.

When we arrived home, Dad said, "Can you believe, someone stole my whiskey and replaced it with water?" Mother never said a word about her prayer. She didn't know that I heard her, but I KNOW that God answered her prayer that day. Years later, Mom told Dad, but I don't think he ever believed her, not until he became a believer.

One might reason that someone stole the whiskey, but I don't buy that. Nothing happens by chance in God's realm of producing miracles. And — who would have taken the time to pour water back into the jug after they stole the moonshine? They would have taken the entire jug with them. Even more convincing is the fact that it was winter. If there had been water in the jug it would have frozen. It just doesn't make sense.

I know one thing for sure. I became a believer that day.

Pictured, left to right, are Allen's brother Ike (Isaac, Jr.) and his wife, Betty, with Allen. Easter Cantrell took the photo. Roy and his mother were sustained in their faith when Moonshine was turned into water as a result of prayer.

Chicken Feathers

A PERSON WHO IS DRUNK can do the weirdest things sometimes. It could not have gotten any stranger than when my drunken father came home one night with two chickens that he had stolen from Mrs. Pennington's chicken house. He tried to hide his crime by burning the feathers in our wood burning cook stove.

Of course Dad didn't dispose of the evidence himself. He woke up Kate and me, and we were instructed how to do it.

First, we had to boil some water to scald the chickens after Dad wrung their necks, and we had to pluck the feather off then singe the fine hairs by holding the chicken over an open flame. Then we were to burn the feather in the stove. Have you ever tried to burn chicken feathers, especially wet ones? They don't burn very well; they just smoke and stink to high heaven.

I'm sure you have seen the program on television where criminals do dumb things and get caught. Well, this was as dumb a thing as they come. If the law had wanted to catch the person who stole Mrs. Pennington's chickens, all they would have had to do was follow the trail of smoke and the disgusting odor of the burnt chicken feathers coming from our house. It would be like tracking someone in the snow from the scene of the crime right to their door. Luckily, no report was made, and no one came looking for two chickens, or Dad would have been sleeping it off in jail.

I don't think we ever got all the feathers burned. The next morning our kitchen looked like a chicken house that had been invaded by some wild animals. There were chicken bones and feathers everywhere, and the air still reeked with the stench of burnt chicken feathers.

Dad sobered up by the next morning and he was horrified at what he had done. But this happened all the time! He would do something dumb and regret it when he sobered up, but there was never a way of undoing his mischief. On one hand Dad wanted to make it right with Mrs. Pennington and pay her for the chickens, but on the other hand he was too embarrassed to admit that he had done such a dumb thing.

We cleaned up the crime scene the best we could, but we couldn't undo the crime itself. He not only stole two chickens, but involved two of his children in the cover up. The stench of the chicken feather finally left our house, but the memory of that night was forever etched in our memory. The sad part for Kate and me was the fact that Dad always taught us to be honest. For us to see him come home with stolen chickens diminished his stature in our eyes.

We found that living with an alcoholic is like being on the wrong side of a two-head coin. It's a no win situation. In the January 2000 issue of the *American Journal of Public Health*, an article appears with new estimates of the number of children of alcoholics. Using data from the 1992 National Longitudinal

Alcohol Epidemiological Survey, the NIAAA authors found that 15% of all United States children were currently exposed to alcohol abuse and/or dependence in the family (which includes any adults living in the household), and 43% of all children were exposed to someone who, during their lifetime, satisfied a diagnosis of alcohol abuse or dependence. Assuming that the best estimate lies between these two extremes, it was determined that approximately 1 in 4 children in the United States is exposed to alcohol abuse and /or dependence in the family at some point before age 18.

Keep in mind that most of these types of surveys do not include alcoholics who are in the military, institutionalized, homeless, or who have refused to participate in the survey.

According to the National Institute on Alcohol Abuse and Alcoholism, nearly 14 millions Americans — 1 in every 13 adults — abuse alcohol or are alcoholic. In addition, 53 percent of men and women in the United States report that one or more of their close relatives have a drinking problem.

The Apostle Paul was not an alcoholic, but he was still under the bondage of sin. And in his bondage, he cried out, "O wretched man that I am! Who shall deliver me from the body of this death?" (Romans 7:24) Then he answered his own questions, "I thank God through Jesus Christ our Lord..." (Verse 25)

I watched my father change from an alcoholic to a teetotaler overnight by the power of God. The alcohol that he once loved, he hated. I realize that most people have a more difficult time getting sober than my father did, but I will say that the only real hope of any alcoholic staying sober is through Jesus Christ. He is the Healer of all our diseases.

God forgave my father of all his sins before he died and "cast them away... and made him a new mind and heart and a new spirit." (Ezekiel 18:31) He did not even leave a trace of one chicken feather.

Who Got My Candy?

⟫◈⟪

IT WAS MY VERY FIRST MOVIE. Our next door neighbors, Paul and Louise Cornet, took me. They had two girls nicknamed "Wickie" and "Nookie" who were about my age. The Cornet's were wonderful people, and I shall never forget their kindness to take me with them to my very first movie.

The theater was located in War, West Virginia, a small town about seven miles away from where we lived. It seemed big to me. I was so memorized by the displays in the store windows that I almost wiped out a couple of parking meters with my body as I walked on the sidewalk toward the theater.

I had never been inside of a movie theater before. I got so carried away with the action, that I stood up in the midst of the excitement and forgot about the seat folding up, so I sat down flat on the floor. I went into the theater with a Hershey bar of chocolate candy and swore someone stole it from me, but I had eaten it sometime during the movie. The evidence was the chocolate on my face.

I guess I wasn't half as excited as a man I heard about who went into a theater for his first time. He was drinking, and when he saw a bald eagle swooping down to get an infant who was left defenseless in a field, he whipped out his pistol and shot the eagle (or should I say the movie screen) several times before anyone could stop him.

When I returned home that night, I could hardly sleep. The movie kept playing over and over in my mind. I was hooked. Even though I had little money and lived several miles from the theater, I would collect copper and scrap iron and sell it to get the fifty cents that it cost for the bus ride, admission, a Coke and a candy bar. I went to the movies every chance I got.

Movies were not only enjoyable for me, but they were an escape from the real world of violence and abuse of an alcoholic father. I always hated to see the words, "The End" appear on the screen, because it meant the end of a few moments of serenity for me and the beginning of chaos when I returned home.

The emotional scars of alcohol abuse never go away. The movies served as a kind of therapy for me because they took my mind away from the pain for a few hours. Any distraction was welcomed, even one as slight as wondering who got my candy bar.

"Not That One... This one!"

A TOOTHACHE CAN BE AN ORDEAL, especially if you live miles from a dentist. Pulling a tooth can be even worse, especially if all you have to pull it with is a pair of wire pliers.

That is what I had to do one day when Dad got a tooth ache. Of course, he was drunk, or he would never have let me do it. I did not want to pull his tooth or anyone else's for that matter, but he insisted. I always had problems pulling my own baby teeth when I was little.

I tried every way in the world to persuade Dad to wait and go to a dentist, but it didn't work. I was the oldest and I was usually recruited for things like this.

Dad pointed with his index finger at the tooth he wanted me to extract. I took the wire pliers and placed them on the tooth I though he wanted me to pull. In fact, I did this several times because I keep "chickening out. " Dad gave me a good scolding and told me I had better bear down, get a good grip and pull his tooth or he would give me a good lashing.

I reached in again with the pliers and took my best grip. I twisted and turned and pulled with all my might, but little happened. I could hear the tooth breaking under the pressure, but I could not get the tooth to come out. Now all the time, Dad was cheering me on to pull harder. I tried my best, but the tooth remained firmly in it place.

Exhausted I pulled my pliers out of Dad's mouth and explained to him that I could not get the tooth to come out. I had damaged it pretty severely by this time. He put his finger in his mouth to examine my progress and said in total disgust, "Not that one, this one." I had been trying to pull out a good tooth. I guess I must have closed my eyes at some point and got hold of the wrong one.

When Dad sobered up, he finally had to get to a dentist and have two teeth pulled instead of one. I suppose the lesson we can learn from this story is that there is no substitute for the real thing.

There are numerous substitutes for the real thing in life – sugar, furs, etc. Many of these substitutes meet the needs of mankind, but there is nothing that can substitute when it comes to meeting the needs of the inner man… the spirit. No drug or alcohol can reach there and met the unmet needs, unhealed hurts and unresolved issues, except God's Only Son Jesus Christ. Everything else is temporary.

The apostle Luke writes in Acts 4:12, "Neither is there salvation in any other; for there is non other name under heaven given among men whereby we must be saved."

Ready Or Not Here I Come

MOST PEOPLE WOULD AGREE that the space age began with the launching of the Russian satellite called Sputnik on October 4, 1957 at 10:28 p.m. Moscow time. But I'd like to contest that. I can personally witness to the fact that the space age, at least for me, began the night I hit our front gate going ninety miles an hour and was launched backward several yards to land spread eagle on my back.

There had been a duel going on between our gate and me. You see, the game I devised was to run as fast as I could, open the gate, then see how far I could get up the porch steps before the gate slammed. The gate's challenge was to slam before I set foot on the first step.

The night prior to my becoming an "astronaut for a day," a neighbor of ours died suddenly in his sleep, and I happened to go over to the house and see the man lying in bed dead. The sight scared me half to death. After that I made it a practice to get home before dark. You would think since I was so scared I would never have stayed out again after dark, but on this night in question I stayed out late watching black and white television and trading comic books. When I realized it was dark, I hurriedly gathered up my comic books and headed home.

I remember running home that night with this huge load of comic books under my arm. When I approached the house of the man who had died, I turned on the after burners. The moon was shining brightly, and I could see very well. At least I though so. However, I soon discovered that fear can blind a person.

I caught a glimpse of the front gate. The gate was made out of strong wire and was flexible like a big spring. I could have sworn that the gate was wide open as I prepared for the home stretch. I was going so fast at this point that the comic strip character "Roadrunner" could not have passed me. In my mind my foot touched the first step of our house, when in reality I was catapulted backward into the air as if shot out of a giant slingshot or circus cannon.

I remember lying there on the ground and seeing up in the heavens a big giant light which I later recognized as the moon. Dazed, I crawled around on the ground gathering up my comic books. I was none the worse for wear except for a few minor bruises here and there. Mainly I was embarrassed because I thought the gate was open when in actuality it was shut.

After I came to my senses, I examined the gate and sure enough it was closed. I couldn't help but wonder if maybe a ghost had pulled a trick on me and closed the gate on purpose. The truth is I just misjudged the situation and could have seriously injured myself, not to mention tearing up the gate in the process.

To me the gate represents the obstacles we all face in life. The secret is how we face them. I learned a few common sense things from the gate experience:

First, don't believe everything you think you see.

Second, there will always be closed gates in life, but go through them head first, not feet first.

And third, life isn't over once you have hit a closed gate. Just get up and gather your scatted, shattered and tattered belongings and go back through and try again just a little smarter the next time.

And, finally, say to your gate, "Gate, ready or not here I come." And this time hopefully you will hear a "slam" instead of a "bam"!

Poison Ivy

MENTION POISON IVY AND I SHIVER. I can't stand the thoughts of ever catching it again. I think my fair complexion is part of my problem, because poison ivy sticks to my skin like Velcro. No kidding! All of my life I have had to be careful to avoid it at all costs. I could identify the plant before I learned to read. However, there were times I caught it and did not have a clue how it happened.

I later learned that poison ivy is a sneaky plant, and it can be spread very easily through touching shoes or clothing that has been exposed to the plant. Even the oil from poison ivy can be transmitted through smoke from burning it, and it can be carried by a pet's fur. All I know is that it starts with swelling and itching, and is followed by red inflammation of pimples and blisters. The painful itching is what resonates in my mind the most. Getting rid of it was the big problem when I was young. Now there are ads that say – "Eliminate all sign of poison Ivy in 72 hours," or "This solution gives itch and pain relief in minutes." Now, they tell me!

When I had to deal with poison ivy I had to conjure up my own treatment. The milkweed plant was supposed to be one remedy. When broken it oozes a milky sticky substance that can be applied directly from the plant onto the affected area.

The best home spun remedy is white shoe polish. When I got a bad case of poison ivy Mother covered me with it, and I came out looking like Casper the Ghost. On one occasion, I even applied gasoline, which I definitely do not recommend. However, I found that one can get several miles per gallon from one application.

My worst poison ivy scare happened when Dad came home drunk one day. He whistled for me to come and get him. He did this often. This particular occasion someone had dropped him off at the top of the hill behind our house. There was a winding path that went up the hill to the main road where he was waiting.

He was so drunk he could hardly stand up, so I put one of his arms around my neck and wrapped my other arm around his waist and we began our pilgrimage down the little dirt trail. An abundance of weeds and poison ivy were growing on each side of the path.

Occasionally, both of us would slip and fall down and when we did, Dad would turn loose of me, clutch the grass or poison ivy nearby, and then grab hold of me again. I asked him to be careful about touching me after handling the poison ivy because he knew how allergic I was to it. My comment must have made him mad.

We had reached the backyard gate where poison ivy was growing all over one of the gatepost. To prove to me that the plant would not hurt anyone, he reached out and got a hand full of it and crammed it into the jaw of his mouth like a chew of tobacco. He began cursing and chewing all at the same time, assuring me that it was harmless. Needless to say I was in total shock at this demonstration.

I thought to myself, *Tomorrow you'll be sorry for what you just did because your mouth will be so swollen you won't be able to eat or drink.*

Wrong! Nothing happened to him! He was truly immune to its affects.

Dad had a God given immunity to poison ivy built inside of his genes, and it prevented him from having an allergic reaction to it. It wasn't anything that he had done to earn or deserve the immunity. It was a gift from God.

But there was something Dad was not immune to, and that was sin. No one is. (Romans 3:23) However, there is an instant cure for sin, and that cure is found in John 3:16. Dad found that remedy in Jesus, and it is called eternal life. (See "The Day Dad Got It") It too is a free gift from God, and moreover it is not earned or deserved. Eternal Life is immunity that the devil can't touch. It is immunity forever!

Pictured is James Allen Cantrell in Second Bottom. In the background are the houses of First botttom, where Mr. Waddell of the "Gorilla" story lived. Roy learned a lesson in etiquette that day.

The Gorilla

—◆—

I LOVED COMIC BOOKS when I was a teenager, and my favorite one was "Tarzan and the Apes." We called them funny books in my day. What always fascinated me was how Tarzan was raised by gorillas. I always dreamed of seeing a real one. But my chances of seeing a real live gorilla were about as remote as seeing a flying saucer, because we lived in a mining camp deep in the hills of West Virginia. But the impossible happened. I finally got the chance to see a gorilla.

One summer a small circus came to our area. I guess the mines must have been going pretty well for them to choose to play our neighborhood, but sure enough they did. The circus set up in the next coal camp about a half mile away on the school playground, gorilla and all. It was the talk of the community. You could get in the circus free, but it cost twenty five cents to see the gorilla. I begged Dad to take me to see it, and he finally agreed.

The time was set for us to go to the circus when Dad got off from work at the mines. When he got home, Mr. Waddell, our neighbor, and his two boys had been invited to go with us. They arrived early and everyone stood around in our front yard talking. Just before we were to leave Dad told me to go inside and get a bucket of water and a dipper so that we could get a drink before we left, because there was no money to spend on soda pop.

When I returned with the water, the first thing I did was take a drink, and then I handed the dipper to Dad. To my utter surprise he told me that we weren't going to the circus. I was devastated, because I had looked forward all day long to seeing the gorilla. The reason I could not go was because I did not offer our guests a drink first. I would rather have had a whipping instead, but my punishment for bad manners was no gorilla.

As I watched them leave for the circus, I felt saddened at the thought of missing my first opportunity to see a live gorilla. The gorilla was so close, yet so far way. It was just out of my reach, as everything else good in life seemed to be.

I think I cried all night over the incident, but it was a good lesson for me. I should have been more considerate of our guests and offered them a drink first, but I was so excited about seeing the gorilla that I didn't think about them. I only thought about myself.

I never forgot that harsh but valuable lesson on etiquette Dad taught me that day. It was something that seeing an 800 pound gorilla could never have done. (Romans 8:28)

My Very Own Football

"CATCH!" DAD SAID, as he threw me a partially inflated football on Christmas morning. I was thrilled to have my very own football. However, there was a slight problem; it needed to be pumped up.

Attached to the side of the football was a needle to inflate it, but there was no pump. Since there was no pump I decided to blow it up myself. I inserted the needle into the ball and blew with all my might - but nothing happened. I found that transferring air from the outside to the inside of a football by mouth is no less than a small miracle. No matter how much I huffed and puffed into the needle, my football remained as squishy as an overripe tomato.

Did you ever try to play with a partially inflated football? It can be done, but it isn't half as much fun as playing with a normal one, and this is where imagination has got to take over. My friends and I played with it until it wore out, but we couldn't pass it very far, and it was always hard to catch. No matter how much fun we had playing football, there was always something missing. That "something" was the fact that the football did not have air in it.

Thinking up alternative ways of doing things always came in handy in my area of Appalachia where I grew up. They say imagination is the largest "nation" in the world. What we weren't able to have in reality, we made up for it in our imaginations.

The missing air in the football is a reminder to me today of the people who are living without Jesus in their lives. They are much like my partially inflated football. Something inside is missing, making life incomplete. When we are born into this world, God says to us what my father said to me that Christmas morning many years ago…"Catch"…and He throws us the gift of life. But something is missing. We are yet incomplete. Life is not complete until we fill it with the necessary ingredient to make it worthwhile.

The "something" that is missing is Jesus. Just as I tried with all my might to inflate my football myself, we too try to fill the emptiness life brings with all sorts of temporal things. Nothing can fill that void until we make a conscious choice to accept Christ as our personal Savior, and only then will we be completely filled.

Ole Rowdy

MY DREAM TO OWN MY OWN DOG came true when I was about thirteen years old. Dad and I visited a friend of his, whose dog had just delivered a litter of puppies. I fell in love with one of them and asked if I could have it.

"Yes, you may have it if you will pay for it," he said.

We really didn't have any money, but I had ten chickens that I had raised from hatchlings. They were about half grown at the time. The man agreed to a deal, and I caught the chickens after they went to roost that night. The next day I took the chickens to the man and swapped them for my own puppy.

I called him "Rowdy" and he wagged his tail and licked my face. I knew we were going to be buddies for life. He looked like a beagle but was about twice the size when he got grown. He had black and tan spots here on a white background with speckles scattered here and there. His eyes were a beautiful brown and full of life. His forehead was flat. Dad said that was important in dogs because it showed they were intelligent and could track animal scents better

Rowdy became my true friend and companion in life. That was especially true when Dad got drunk, and he was drunk a lot. When he did something to make me feel sad or fearful, I would go into the nearby woods and sit and talk to Rowdy. I declare I think he understood what I was saying. He would sniff, wag his tail and nod his head now and then when I explained my problems to him. At least I felt better after our conversations. I would give him a big hug, and we would go back home into the real world of fear and confusion.

Words can't express in words how much Rowdy meant to me. A person could not have been anymore important in my life. We ate, slept, and hunted together. He was my best friend. Our relationship lasted until I was eighteen years old. Then, what I feared for years came to pass.

I had just accepted Christ into my life, and everything was wonderful. Then, out of the clear blue, Dad came home drunk one day with two men and informed me that he had sold "Ole Rowdy."

We lived up in a holler that forked off of the main road that was impassable with a car. So the two men sat in the car and waited for my dad to get Rowdy for them. One of the men I knew well. He had wanted to buy my dog for years, but I wouldn't have sold him for any amount of money — not even a million dollars, and I'm not kidding. How does one put a price on a member of the family? That's how close "Ole Rowdy" and I were.

I heard Dad call my name as he came up the path to our house, and I came out to meet him. He had his belt in his hand, and he told me to take the belt and put it around Rowdy's neck. I was to take him to the men at the mouth of the holler because he had sold him for a sixteen gauge shotgun and a half gallon of moonshine.

I should not have been shocked at what he had done, because he had pulled crazy stunts like this before. Nevertheless, I felt I was having a nightmare and would wake up soon and all this would not be true. But it was true. My first impulse was to defy my father and not do what he asked of me, but on the other hand, I respected him as my dad no matter how I felt about the situation. I thought about the commandment in the Bible that said children should honor their father and mother. I didn't want to go against the Bible. (Exodus 20:12)

I went to the car and explained to the man who had traded for Rowdy that Dad was drunk, and that he was my dog. I said that Dad didn't know what he was doing. The man wouldn't listen. I begged him not to take "Ole Rowdy," but he just laughed at me.

I went back up toward the house calling "Ole Rowdy," and he came to meet me. At a beautiful spot under a big shady tree I sat down on a log and called him to me. He reared up on my legs and extended his paws in a form of embrace with his tongue panting. He looked at me with those brown enquiring eyes as if to say, "What's up?"

Tears began to flow down my face as I shared how I loved him and how I cherished our time together. We were best buddies. If you saw one of us, you saw the other one. I explained what had happened and that as a Christian I had to honor my father's request. I said, "Rowdy, you know how much I love you and how you have been my best friend all these years, but I have a new best friend, and His name is Jesus."

We walked slowly to where the car was parked at the bottom of the hill. Again I pleaded with the man not to take my dog, but he pulled Rowdy into the car and drove away. My heart ached; the tears wouldn't stop. I turned around as the car disappeared out of sight and I waved, "Goodbye, Old Friend."

Note: I never saw Rowdy again. A few weeks later, Mother saw the son of the man who bought him. When she asked about Rowdy, he said that they regretted buying him because he refused to eat or hunt. He eventually died, apparently from grief and starvation.

Revival Time is Here

GOD CALLS YOU TODAY

"TODAY if ye will hear His voice harden not your hearts." Heb. 3:7-8.

"Seek ye the Lord while He may be found, call ye upon Him while He is near." Is. 55:6.

"Behold NOW is the accepted time;behold, NOW is the day of salvation." II Cor. 6:2.

Evangelist, James Earls-Gospel Preacher for twenty-five years, in various states.

Services: Place: *Newhall Church*

Time: 7:30 PM

E V E R Y O N E   W E L C O M E

It was the Evangelist James Earles who gave the author's mother the keys to the church at Newhall.

Church On Fire

THE DAY MOTHER BECAME A CHRISTIAN was the day salvation came to our home. Without Mother's commitment to Christ I don't know what would have happened to our family.

Her conversion actually came about as the result of a challenge from Dad to go to a local revival meeting for the purpose of finding fault with the church's style of worship and to make fun of the woman evangelist. Dad and Mother were strictly against women preachers. The plan was to return home with the juicy gossip about what happened at church, but alas, just the opposite happened.

Mother came home alright but with a testimony of her own of how God had saved her. She informed Dad that she was going back the next night for more. You can imagine how this news upset him. He had lost his partner in crime and he was not a happy camper. In fact, he was so infuriated at her conversion to Christianity that he spent most of their married life persecuting her. However, his attacks on her faith didn't diminish her zeal for God at all; they seemed only to fuel the fire of determination to do even more.

The coal company built the community which consisted of a school, store and houses, and also a church. The church was located at the end of the grade school grounds, but it stayed empty most of the time. The area was so poor that there wasn't enough money for pastoral support. It had changed hands several times. The Methodists occupied it for a while and then the Assembly of God. The church doors stayed locked most of the time. After Mother got saved she had a desired to open the church doors, but she didn't have the keys.

One night she dreamed that the little church was on fire. She could see the flames and hot coals engulfing the church. "Lord," she prayed, "don't let our church burn down. If you will let me live and give me the opportunity to open the church and have Sunday school, I'll do it." When she awoke, she was praying this prayer aloud.

Shortly after her dream, an evangelist came for a revival. Mother and the evangelist were the only ones in attendance. They spent several days, just the two of them, praying for a revival to come to the community. She said that when the two of them prayed it sounded as if there were a house full of people praying. No one else showed up for the revival, so the evangelist left town, but before he did, he handed the church keys to Mother and said, "Mrs. Cantrell, I was told to leave the church keys with you." This was an answer to her prayer in her dream.

Mother took the keys and opened the church the next Sunday. She invited her next door neighbor who brought her two girls and Mother took her three girls, Kate, Dora and Zetta, which made a total of seven attendees in all. The next Sunday there were fourteen, and the next Sunday there were twenty-one who turned out. The church began to grow very rapidly to an attendance of 102 in a six months period.

The church growth began in a strange way. One night Mother decided to lead the singing, and a group of girls in attendance laughed at her. She broke down and wept at the girls' disrespect. When the girls saw how they had offended Mother, the Holy Spirit convicted them for making fun of her, and they went forward and prayed to receive Christ. One of the girls became the pianist of the church, and the other girls helped with the music. The core leadership of the church was birthed over the episode that evening.

Shortly after the church's burst of growth, a pastor by the name of Reverend Lyons and his family came to pastor the church. Mother continued to teach Sunday school there for three and one half years, until she moved too far away to attend there.

The little church made an impact on the community as a whole and on my life personally. One night several of us boys attended the meeting mainly to meet girls. When the minister finished his sermon, he made his way back to where several of us boys were seated on a pew together. He began with the first one and went down the pew asking each one of us if we were saved. Everyone except me answered in the affirmative. I remember saying "No" to the question because I had not made a commitment to Christ. However, I remember how badly I felt afterwards. It was the first time I realized I was lost and needed a Savior. It was the turning point in my life.

Mother is eight-four years old now and she still has the fire of the Holy Spirit burning in her. She is one of the best personal soul winners I have ever seen. The church in her dream did burn, but not literally. It burned with revival fire that never went out in her life or in the lives of those who experienced the revival fire of those days when God showed up as a consuming fire.

After Dad died, Mother and we seven children went back to West Virginia to visit. We went to the site of the church that she had opened and where she had taught Sunday school many years ago, but it was gone. Then, we went to the little church where she got saved in March 1950. She excitedly rehearsed the events of the night she knelt at the church's altar and gave her heart to God. Her conversion was so dynamic that it impacted all of our lives; including Dad's.

A Sunday school class from the little church where Easter led the rebuilding of the congregation from zero to over 100.

The Kitten With Ten Lives

I DEBATED OVER WHETHER OR NOT to include this story in the book because it is so gruesome, but it witnesses of God's power so strongly that I felt it was worth telling.

This incident occurred on a cold winter night. I don't know what set Dad off this time, but in reality it didn't take much to upset him when he was drunk. The slightest things could trigger his anger and cruelty. Usually if something upset him when he was sober, he waited until he got drunk to take revenge in some shape, form or fashion. I think the alcohol gave him the courage to confront whatever bothered him.

We all knew that Dad despised cats. All our lives he told us stories about how cats were evil. He would not allow cats in or around the house. The only reason he would tolerate one was to get rid of mice. This must have been the reason we had a little kitten in the house the night this happened. It was a bluish grey color, and Mother had named her "Blue."

This particular evening he again came home in a drunken state. While we were sitting talking, the little grey kitten came up to Dad and rubbed up against him like cats will do. It made him angry. He reached down and picked up the kitten and clamped his knees around its head. He picked up my Scout hatchet next to him and began to beat the kitten in the head as hard as he could with the blunt end of it. He then released the kitten, and it fell to the floor lifeless.

Dad said to me, "Get it out of here."

I picked up the kitten and took it outside. We lived in the last house of a mining camp at the edge of a creek that wrapped around our front yard. I walked out to the bank of the creek holding the kitten by it's hind legs, and I threw it with all my strength out onto the frozen creek and sadly walked back into the house.

I am so thankful to remember a godly mother whose prayers saved us, as well as many animals, from serious injury. The next morning Dad had sobered up and as usual was shaking from an alcohol hangover. He was in no shape to confront what happened next.

We heard a "meow" at the front door, and when we opened it, there was the same kitten wanting inside. We examined it all over, and it did not have a bump on its head or a scratch on its body. It was an absolute miracle. Dad became very nervous and he told me to get the kitten some cream and feed it. He kept the cat the rest of its life and would not have taken anything for it after that. I think he was afraid that God would strike him down if he did any more harm to it.

As Paul Harvey says, "Now for the rest of the story..."

Not long afterwards, the mining company closed the mines where Dad worked and they sold the company houses. Dad refused to buy the house we lived in, so we had to move to a rented house a couple of miles away. When we moved, the kitten that now had become a cat, was no where to be found, so we had to leave her behind.

One day out of no where the cat showed up with a new born kitten in her mouth. A day later she came with another one, and a day later another kitten. She found us somehow and carried her three kittens, one by one, across a mountain to join us at our new location. I have often thought how much that cat must have loved us and wanted to be a part of our family to travel so far, especially after Dad tried to kill her. If only people could be as forgiving!

This is not the only miracle I saw God perform in our family. His presence was real every day. When I look back now and think about what we went through, I know that the kitten wasn't the only one with ten lives.

Two mother cats with their kittens in a cardboard box

"Snake Bit"

—⟫◆⟪—

"SNAKE BIT" WAS ONE of the most dreaded phrases a person could hear when I was a boy because it was a life threatening event, and doctors were few and far between.

We were taught from a young age to be careful and watch out for snakes when we were in the woods hunting or picking berries. We knew what every poisonous snake looked like and how to avoid them at all cost.

I thought I knew what to do in case I got bit because I was a Boy Scout, and they taught me to make two "X" cuts across each fang puncture with my Scout knife. I remember sharpening my knife this particular morning before going blackberry picking to be prepared just in case I did get bit. I wish that I could report that all this preparation made a big difference, but it didn't.

I took my dog Rowdy with me, and a couple of other dogs joined us as we went through the mining camp up by the grade school. We went past the place where I dug a human skull from the dirt bank behind the school one day while playing in the dirt. It was a skull of a child. I was told that an Indian grave yard must have been there before they excavated to build the school.

The dogs and I climbed the hill in back of the school and crossed the strip mining road that cut a road around the mountain for trucks to haul coal out. I crossed an old rail fence into our garden where Dad and I had dug up the ground to plant a few vegetables. I was headed for the blackberry patch at the rear of the clearing.

I cautiously made my way into the berry patch with a small dipper in my hand to pick berries. I set my two-gallon bucket down close by to pour my berries into after I filled the dipper. The dogs were busily sniffing for rabbits under the briar patch, so I though if there was a snake they would scare it away. I was wrong. I guess the berries were so plentiful and beautiful that I got carried away picking them and forgot to look for a snake. I placed my left foot firmly in place so I could push forward with my right foot to reach the berries better. When I eased forward to pick the berries, my movement caused the copperhead to strike.

I knew immediately I had been bitten by a snake. It felt like a hypodermic needle about six inches long stuck into my leg. It was very painful. I glanced down at the ground where my foot was, and I saw the tail half of a copperhead slithering away. It happened in a split second. Then I panicked.

I ran back down the way I came as fast as I could go. Later Dad retraced my steps by the things I left behind. He found the bucket where I left it with berries still in it. The dipper I dropped at the fence when I went over it in one giant leap. I never once though of cutting the fang marks with my pocket knife. Now I think doctors advise against it so the Lord was protecting me even then.

I ran past the school back down to the mining camp where a woman was ironing on the front porch. I ran up to the fence and yelled out to her that I had been bitten by a copperhead. She immediately yanked the ironing cord out of the drop socket hanging from the front porch ceiling.

She hurried me into her car, and off we went to the local company doctor's office. He was not in. So she decided to take me home to pick up my mother which was on our way to the next nearest doctor. Being a Christian and believed in prayer, Mother began immediately to pray for me.

We drove several miles to the next doctor's office, and he was not in. So we turned around and went to the next town and although they were in, they did not have any anti-venom. The doctor recommended that they take me to the hospital in the next town. On the way to the hospital we ran into road construction and we were held up until we were able to tell one of the workers our emergency. They escorted us around the traffic and notified the hospital of our urgent situation.

As soon as I arrived at the hospital, the medical staff rushed me to the emergency room where they gave me thirteen shots all over my body and kept me in the Richlands, Virginia hospital for three day. I had a lot of swelling, and it took months to completely heal. I will always carry the scars as a reminder of what happened that day.

All of mankind has been snake bit by that Old Serpent, the Devil. He bit our parents Adam and Eve in the Garden of Eden and, as a result, all of mankind has carried his deadly venom ever since. The good news is that Jesus Christ came and bruised his head and provided us with the anti-venom to counteract his deadly poison. That anti-venom is the precious blood of Jesus Christ.

Monkeyshines

ONCE A YEAR WE WENT ON VACATION back to Kentucky where we had migrated from to West Virginia so that Dad could find work in the coal mines. It was only a 120 mile trip, but it seemed as though we were traveling to some distant land due to all the preparation we went through before leaving.

Vacation meant we got some new clothes at the Company Store. One hundred dollars would buy clothes for the whole family — new shoes, shirts, trousers, socks, blouses and skirts, and Dad always got a new hat.

We never owned a car except for one that Dad won in a poker game. He only kept it for three days and then sold it for two hogs and some whiskey. He never drove a car in his entire life. Mother got her driver's license when she was nearly sixty-five years old. She was the only one of six girls in her family to drive a car.

When we went on vacation we hired someone to drive us. This particular year Dad hired the man next door. He had just bought a brand new Henry J automobile. It was baby blue with two fins sticking up like wings on the rear fender. Kate always got car sick and she stuck her head out of the window and regurgitated all the way to Kentucky. She looked a greenish gray by the time we arrived at our destination

We stopped about half way on the trip to get some gas and snacks and go to the rest room. The owner of the store had three monkeys in a large cage on the outside of the store to attract customers. Dad was pretty drunk by this time, and he decided to go to the cage and pet the baby money. The two adults were at the opposite end of the cage watching over their baby.

The baby monkey was very friendly and came to greet Dad as he approached the cage. When Dad reached in to pet the baby monkey, the mother monkey sprang into action. As fast as lightening, she leaped across the cage, and in one stroke scratched his face from his hairline across his eye lid down to his chin.

Dad was very upset to say the least. He shook the monkeys' cage with all his might, and tried to get to them to retaliate but to no avail. He even went inside and tried to buy the monkeys so he could kill them, at least the two adults who had assaulted him. Nothing worked, so we left.

There was an unwritten code of the mountains that said laughter was a sin, or close to it, and it was usually not tolerated by parents for very long. Children were told that if they laughed something bad would happen, and their laughter would turn into crying. What a terrible rule to impose on children who should grow up with their lives filled with fun and laughter.

However, when Dad got scratched by the monkey, the incident was so funny we had to laugh even if it meant facing a firing squad. What made it so funny was the way the scratch on Dad's eyelid appeared and disappeared when he blinked his eye. When he blinked the scratch lines connected above and below the eye. I don't know why this was so funny to us children, but it was hilarious.

Of course, we couldn't let Dad know that we were laughing at him, or we would have gotten a whipping for sure. To mask what we were laughing at, we would point out the window as if we were laughing at something outside. This made it even funnier. Dad never caught on to what was so funny. It was the most fun we had on the entire vacation.

I guess the moral of this story is that even in the worst of circumstances in life, God has a way of bringing laughter into our lives in the blink of an eye.

The monkey that scratched Allen Cantrell's face was in a larger cage located beside these cages where the children are looking at other animals.

A Brand New Bicycle

MY VERY FIRST BICYCLE was anything but new. It was what one would call a "Hines 57" model assembled from old spare parts of a dozen discarded bicycles that I found here and there or traded for. It had no fenders and slung mud everywhere when it rained. The sprocket chain slipped off at every turn. But it was all I had up until Dad bought me a brand new one.

A new bicycle was something I had dreamed about ever since I was old enough to ride one. My dream came true one day when Dad bought me a brand new red bicycle from the company store. It was the only one they had, and it didn't matter that it was designed for a girl. I had my own bike, and I was proud of it.

That summer when vacation time came, we took my bicycle with us. There was no room for it in the car trunk because it was full of our clothes and a few little hand-made gifts for family members. We took the bicycle apart and held the frame and wheels in our laps in the back seat.

When we arrived at Grandpa and Grandma's house, I put the bicycle back together again. After a day at Mother's parent's Dad decided to take me over to his parents for a visit. We caught a ride over there and put the bicycle in the car trunk. We stayed until after dark and returned with Dad walking and me riding my bike. Dad was too drunk to ride anything.

He was fussing because he didn't have any whiskey or money to buy any. He always gambled away all of his money the first day we were on vacation. I remember one time when Dad passed out on the porch, and Mother asked me to search his pockets for money. I found one dime.

That evening, Dad ran across some people he knew who had whiskey. Even though I was barley a teenager I knew what was coming next. He was going to sell my bicycle for whiskey, and that was what happened. I have often wondered how grown-ups could take things away from children – things such as my bicycle – when they knew taking them was breaking the child's heart. But I figured alcohol works on the buyer the same as it does on the seller. They both just don't have any feelings when they are intoxicated.

I dared not show any emotions when Dad sold my bicycle. I hid the tears from him. I just held it all in and pretended that it was okay to trade my bicycle for whiskey for him. Children of alcoholics learn to be great pretenders. This was not the first time he had sold something dear to me to support his habit, and it would not be the last. (See "Ole Rowdy")

There is an ancient Chinese proverb that says "In a broken nest, there are few whole eggs." I suppose that in some alcoholic "nests" there are more broken than others, and some "eggs" from those nests are less whole than others. I'm not sure about that, but what I do know is that every "egg" in every broken "nest" is salvageable by God's love and grace. I know from experience that this broken "egg" that came from a broken "nest" was put back together again, and that is something that all the king's horses and all the kings men could not do for Humpty Dumpty. But Jesus could for me! And he did.

Permission to kill

WHEN I WAS A CHILD, guns were a part of my life. News of someone getting shot or killed was received as a normal event. One of my grandfathers killed a man and shot others. My uncle was killed out of revenge. My father was shot by his cousin for no reason. I remember the news coming to us via the grapevine. There were no telephones. The news started at the place of the shooting and traveled from house to house, two miles, until it reached us. It was awful scary to hear that my dad had been shot and possibly killed.

Even though he had been shot in the upper part of his leg, by the time the story got to us, he had been "shot in the chest several times." Dad said he was sitting down on an embankment, and his cousin pulled out his gun and aimed at him. If he had not stood up the bullet would have hit him in the chest. All of them were drinking when the incident occurred.

As I grew up I was taught how to use guns and told to protect myself, even to the point of killing someone if threatened. I vividly remember Dad giving me permission to kill one day.

He was drinking with his buddies, and they had stopped along the railroad to gamble. They found a comfortable place just inside the trees out of sight. Invariably a fight would break out over cheating at cards, and sometimes one of them would get seriously hurt. I was told by my dad if a fight broke out to shoot whoever jumped on him.

I remember sitting on a rock a few yards away with my loaded 22 rifle on my lap poised to shoot anyone who jumped on my dad. The sad part is that I got bored sitting there waiting and actually wanted a fight to break out so I could shoot someone. There is no doubt in my mind I would have shot the person who started a fight. The though still frightens me to this day.

These are the situations that alcoholics put there children in that they might not do otherwise if it were not for the whiskey. I look back now and believe with all my heart that it was God's protection that kept me from taking another person's life over a brawl at a card game.

Alcoholics don't realize until it's too late what danger they put themselves in and how they endanger others, especially their families. One time Dad set the woods on fire behind our house, and it became a major fire. Firefighters were called out to fight it. It took days to put it out. I was hired as well as others to fight it, and one of us could have gotten killed.

An alcoholic will do things that may not be harmful but makes no sense at all. There was the time Dad killed two half grown hogs in mid summer because he wanted to satisfy a craving for pork. We had no refrigerator and most of the meat ruined before we could eat it. Then when winter came there was no meat for the family.

My advice to anyone who has not taken a drink of alcohol is DON'T! I'm speaking from experience. The Bible says, "It bites like a serpent, and stings like an adder." (Proverbs 23:32)

No More Bananas, Please!

———◆———

THE ONE BRIGHT SPOT in Dad's drinking was that he always managed to come home with something to eat when he got drunk. We would be down to our last bean in the cupboard, and without a penny in his pocket he always managed to come home with something good to eat. Not beans and such, but real food such as soda pop or bananas.

We knew what the expression "poor as Job's turkey" meant. We didn't get sweets or fruits very often. Usually those were delicacies only obtainable at Christmastime. If we got them at other times, we picked them out of the dump where the company store discarded their overripe fruit, vegetables and worm infested sweets. I remember my sister Kate came to me with a whole box of Hershey bars with almonds that she had picked up at the dump. She was thrilled with her find, which was evidenced by the chocolate on her face, until I pointed out the bugs in the almonds.

Writing this book about our life has brought back some bad memories, but some funny ones also. We have laughed about Kate licking the glass counter at the company store where the candy was displayed. She had a big imagination. We each had to have one to survive.

Then there was the time Dad brought home several cases of soda pop of every flavor in the store. I drank at least one of every variety and hid as many as I could between the logs of the log cabin. I found soda pop for weeks afterwards where I had hid them. However, when Dad brought home the stalk of bananas that was the biggest treat of all.

I though only rich people ate bananas until Dad came home one night with a whole stalk of them. I mean there must have been a hundred bananas on the thing. It was all he could carry. You should have seen the excitement in the house. We were like little monkeys greeting Tarzan of the jungle.

I went bonkers. I ate every banana I could hold and more. I ate them for breakfast, lunch and dinner. Those I couldn't eat, I hid. And many of them I never found again. Those I didn't find probably became "happy meals" for rodents. I got so sick of bananas that I never wanted to see another one again. Even the pictures of them made me ill.

However, I learned an important lesson the night Dad brought home the stalk of bananas. That is this: alcohol is not the only thing that one can overindulge in. Conversely, the big difference is that alcohol is addictive, and bananas aren't.

But no more bananas, please!

Tree House

⟫◆⟪

THERE ARE SOME THINGS IN LIFE that gives us comfort, and they can be as simple as a tree house. This was the case for me when I was a young man. My tree house was my place of escape from a world of alcoholism.

There was a huge beech tree not too far from where we lived, and it was a perfect place to build a tree house. Its limbs reached out from the trunk in a majestic manner and were in the shape of huge cupped hands ready to embrace a boy's loneliness, pain and even his dreams. It was a perfect hiding place for me when I needed to escape the terror at home.

To build my tree house, I took my trusty Scout hatchet and cut down several small saplings and carried them to the base of the tree until I had enough to begin. I tied each one of them with a rope and then tied the other end of the rope around my waist and climbed the tree. I pulled the poles up to the place I wanted to begin, nailed the first one into place, and repeated the process until I completed the floor. I left an opening in the floor so I could crawl up through it to finish the rest of the tree house. It was a lot of fun.

When things got unbearable at home I would go to my tree house and just sit there alone, secure away from everything. I felt safe there, much like a squirrel nestled in its nest of leaves high atop a tree. Some time I would day dream that I was a space cadet ready to be blasted off to the moon or to some other far off place in outer space. Or, I imagined that I was Jack on the beanstalk and would come down one day with a whole bag of golden eggs to buy whatever I wanted. And, then, I would take my Scout hatchet and chop down the beanstalk and get rid of the big bad giant who was chasing me.

The day when my tree house became my very best friend was when Dad broke my 22 rifle by hitting it again and again on a rock in the back yard. (See "The Fire That Won't Go Out.") He was drinking as usual and he wanted his shot gun shells. I didn't know where they were, so he took out his anger on me and smashed my gun. It was the gun I killed my first squirrel with when I was sixteen, right where I built my tree house. To commemorate the occasion I carved a squirrel on the stock. My 22 was the only thing I owned except Ole Rowdy, my dog. When I saw the pieces of my gun scattered everywhere, I did something I had never done before.

I had never even talked back to Dad for seventeen years of my life. But that day I cursed my father with every vulgar word that I had learned from him or anyone else up to that point. I took Rowdy and ran away crying. When I got to the edge of the woods, I glanced over my shoulder and saw my father with his shot gun up to his shoulder aiming it at me. I thought he had found his shotgun shells and was going to shoot me. Apparently Dad was just faking it when he aimed his gun at me, or it was the mercy of God that he didn't shoot.

I ran into the woods and climbed up into my tree house, crying and confused but safe. I was devastated more over what I had said to my father than over what had happened to my gun. I knew that I could not return home without getting a severe beating for defying him. I sat there pondering what to do when I heard my best friend, James Pennington, call my name.

He delivered newspapers and he had gone to the house looking for me. When he couldn't find me, he knew where I would be. I explained to him what had happened, and he invited me to spend the night at his house. I climbed down and went with him, never to see my tree house again.

After Dad died, Mother and all of us children went back to West Virginia for a visit and to find some closure. On my list was a visit to my old friend the tree house.

The old beach tree was still standing with visible nail scares on the side of the tree where I had nailed stair steps to climb up. But there was no sign of a tree house. It had rotted and fallen to the ground a long time ago. I found a small piece of wood with a nail in it that I brought home for a souvenir.

I, like the old beach tree, have a few scars left from all the emotional trauma that I suffered as a child. But like my tree house that disappeared with time, my memories of the past have vanished except for a souvenir or two that I have purposely keep as a reminder of God's Amazing Grace. It has been said that time heals all wounds, but I think the Old Latin Proverb says it best: *Veritatum dies aperit.* "Time discovers all truth."

The Truth I found was through Jesus who said, "I am the way, the truth and the life; no man cometh to the Father, but by me." (John 14:6)

In the lower left of this photograph sits the rock on which Dad broke my 22 rifle to pieces. In the background can be seen the drive-in movie screen and the little community of Cucumber, West Virginia.

The Fire That Won't Go Out!

⟫◆⟪

LIKE MOSES' BURNING BUSH that would not go out, there was an unquenchable fire for learning ignited in my soul the day that Dad burned my school books.

It happened in the fall before my senior year of high school. That summer things were bad at our house. My mother was forced to leave home and take the baby with her to stay with her mother for a few weeks until Dad settled down from his alcohol binge This left five of us children at home with Dad. There were four girls and me.

One day, while he was drunk, Dad was playing with his twelve gauge shotgun and it accidentally went off and barely missed us. He shot a huge hole in the kitchen screen door. It scared him so bad that he told Kate to hide the shotgun shells from him. She did.

The next day when everyone was in school except me, he decided that he wanted the shells, and he asked me for them. I tried to explain to him that I didn't know where they were, but he went into a rage and picked up my 22 rifle and smashed it. Then after he had destroyed my rifle, he began to curse me and threatening to whip me. The Bible says for parents not to provoke their children to wrath, but that is what happened in this case.

I ran off and my best friend James invited me to go home with him. His mother, Lola Pennington, was very understanding and asked me what I was going to do. I told her that I wanted to go to my grandmother's house where my mother and baby brother were staying. The next morning Mrs. Pennington packed me a lunch and gave me a toothbrush and two dollars. She took me to the West Virginia and Kentucky state line and let me out there so I could hitchhike. I caught a coal truck on top of Bradshaw Mountain, and the driver took me most of the way. I walked the last few miles to Grandpa and Grandma Potter's house.

When I arrived, Mother was shocked to see me. I told her what had happened and that I could not return home. She was heart broken at what had happened and immediately returned home to make sure the other children were all right.

My grandparents agreed to keep me the rest of the summer and let me enroll in High School. That fall Mother wrote asking me to come home. I explained that I could not return home unless Dad agreed to it. One day a letter came from her saying that she had bought some used high school books for me and that Dad said that it was alright for me to return and go to school. I was thrilled.

My uncle Scooter took me back to West Virginia so I could enroll in school. When I arrived, Dad was drunk, and he brought up the incident that caused me to leave. He instructed my mother to go and get the books she had bought. She brought them to me, and Dad said for me to put them in the yard near the big rock that he broke my gun on. I obeyed him and he gathered up some paper and lit a fire to the books. I watched them burn! I knew that I couldn't stay there and go to school. Uncle Scooter told me that it would be better if I went back with him to Grandmother's house. I did.

I was angry at my father for burning my school books that day, but something good came out of it. My father didn't know it, but he ignited two fires. One fire burned my books and went out shortly afterwards. The other fire ignited an unquenchable thirst for learning that continues to burn within me even to this day.

What I am about to share now is to give honor to God for his faithfulness. Dad and I reconciled after he burned my school books. He lost his job in the coal mines in West Virginia, and the family had to move back to Kentucky where I was living with my grandmother. I finished my senior year at home with my family.

Ever since the day my books were burned I realized their value and the value of a good education. The fire of learning still burns as brightly as ever as I envision the remnant of my high school life smoldering in the recesses of my memory.

To God is the glory!

Grandma's Bank

NO ONE KNEW WHERE GRANDMA KEPT HER MONEY except Pa. That is, not until that fateful night when the bank went bust because the "stud" tobacco sack she kept her money in came untied from her petty coat strap and disappeared into the night.

After the great depression, very few people kept their money in banks, especially in our neck of the woods. What little money we managed to save went into some kind of personal safekeeping such as our shoes, mayonnaise jars, or tied to ones undergarments. Pa had trusted in Grandma's bank for many a year without loosing a cent. That is until that night the knot came untied on her underwear, and the bank went broke.

It was grandma's habit to check her bank roll occasionally by feeling for the tobacco bag located near her bosom. Sometime during the night she felt for the money bag, and it was not there. I can imagine the panic that overwhelmed her as she realized that she had lost their life savings in one fell swoop.

Grandma awoke my cousin, Ira, and me and asked us if we had seen her money. She described the tobacco bag and told us how much money was in it. It was in the hundreds of dollars. We assured her that we had not seen the money. We dressed as quickly as possible, got a flashlight and set out to retrace Grandma's steps of the previous day.

Ira, who is a medical doctor now, was more like a son to Grandpa and Grandma, because they had raised him from an infant. I knew that they trusted him, but I was not sure they trusted me, because I had only arrived a few months earlier to stay with them to complete my final year of high school.

We decided to begin the search at the barn where she milked the cow, then go over to the hog pen where she fed them some weeds she pulled from the garden earlier, then, back to the smoke house. We found nothing! We went back again and again shining the flash light from side to side, checking out everything that resembled the "stud" tobacco bag, but the little money bag was no where to be found.

We decided to take a closer look near the water well located adjacent to the back porch. On our left we passed two water buckets sitting on a board shelf that was nailed between two porch posts. It was customary in those days to drink water from buckets using a long-handle dipper. Anybody who was thirsty put the dipper into the bucket and took a drink. It wasn't very sanitary, but no one seemed to mind.

Directly in front of us sitting on the back porch was an old Maytag washing machine (See "Grandma's Maytag Miracle") that Grandma used faithfully to wash our clothes. It was hooked up to a drop socket hanging from the porch ceiling. Next to the wall was a wooden box where a hen had chosen to make her nest. To get to the hen's nest one had to reach over the washing machine. That evening Grandma must have reached across the washing machine to get the eggs from the nest. When she pulled in her stomach and stretched to get the eggs, evidently the tobacco bag dropped onto the porch floor.

Grandma couldn't believe she had lost the money because she always kept an apron tied around her below where she had the money tied to her petticoat. She was a plump little woman with a dough boy tummy, and it didn't seem possible for anything to get past her mid-drift. To do so would be something like the proverbial camel passing through a needle's eye.

I never forgot that incident and was relieved that the money was found. I was relieved not just for the money's sake, but also that my grandparents would know that I could be trusted in case they had any doubts.

I graduated from high school and went on to college and seminary, earning a Doctor of Ministry degree and a Ph.D. in Christian counseling. It took me 40 years to earn the degrees due to a lack of funds and being moved from one church assignment to another. Grandma never knew about it, but without her I probably would not have graduated from high school. She died at 102 years old while living with her daughter, my mother. She was alert up until the time she died. She was still making quilts at 100-plus years old and could thread her own needle without eyeglasses.

I preached Grandma's funeral and thought about that night we looked for the little tobacco bag of money that she lost. I thought about how she was no longer keeper of the bank tied to her petticoat. She had been a good steward over what little she had while here on earth and now there was a reward laid up for her in heaven.

I could almost hear Jesus saying to her, "Kate, You have been faithful over a few things. I will make you ruler of many things. Enter into the joys of the Lord."

Thank you, Grandma, for loving me unconditionally!

The home in Shelby Gap, Kentucky that Grandma Potter bought for $1200 with the profits from moonshine whiskey. It was here her "bank" was temporarily lost. Roy killed his "almost miracle rabbit" on the ridge in the background, and the "Maytag Miracle" was on the back porch. He and his cousin Ira attempted to clear the fields around the house using nothing but axes. Their grandpa taught them a valuable lesson when he traded Roy a watch for the money Roy had earned for the work.

The homplace was purchsed in 1943. By 1966 it had appreciated 100%.

Grandpa's Lesson On Trading

⋙◆⋘

DID YOU EVER MESS UP ROYALLY and wish that you could go back and get another chance at making things better? I have more times than I wish to recall. One of those times was when I was making a deal with my grandfather for a watch.

My grandfather hired my cousin, Ira, and me to clear a pasture field for him. We were to cut down all the small saplings in the field so that the grass could grow and furnish food for the farm animals.

Pa said that he would pay us $15 each when the job was finished. The only problem with the deal was that it was impossible for two grown experienced people to clear such a large piece of land with an ax, but we didn't know it. We didn't have the modern equipment such as chain saws, just axes, but we gave it our best effort.

We set out in dead earnest to clear the field. We worked all day and went home in the evening and looked back at our day's labor. The spot was located on the hillside adjacent to the home place. You couldn't see where we had been. We went back again and again cutting down bushes to clear the pasture, but we hardly made a dent in it. The only thing we had to show for our labor was blistered sore hands and bruised egos. The bushes grew faster than we could keep them cut down.

We went to Grandma to plead our case. She knew how to handle Pa because she came back with positive results. Pa agreed to pay us the full amount because he said that we had earned it. However, being the trader he was, we weren't off the hook yet. He called me to where he was sitting in his favorite chair. Close by were all his store of guns, knives and watches that he traded every day to make a living. What he didn't have in the house to trade were either live animals in the pasture or corn whiskey in the cellar. He was the best trader I ever saw. Like a magician working his magic, Pa got back my fifteen dollars pay without me ever seeing it. He knew exactly how to do it.

He took out a shinny used seventeen-jewel Bulova wrist watch and said, "Try this on."

It had an expansion band and all. I loved it. He offered to sell it to me for fifteen dollars. It was the amount of money that he owed me for helping to clear the pasture. I quickly agreed to the deal, and then he said something important to me.

"Roy, I would have taken ten dollars for the watch if you had bargained with me."

I readily agreed, thinking he was offering to start the process all over. "O.K," I said. " I'll give you ten dollars for the watch."

"No!" Pa said firmly. "I want to teach you a lesson on trading. Don't ever make an offer on something. Always let the other person quote their price to you first and then bargain with them for a lower price." He continued, "I have learned that most people ask more than what the item is worth in the beginning so they can have room to go down on the price. If you give the asking price, you are giving more than the item is worth." Pa was a firm man and I knew that I had bought me a $15.00 watch.

I never forgot the lesson that Pa taught me that day. The watch cost me five dollars extra, but the lesson has saved me thousands of dollars since then. I kept the watch. It doesn't kept time anymore, but I keep it in my jewelry box and ever now and then I will go and take it out and just hold it and reflect on the time when Pa taught me that important lesson on trading.

The old watch means more to me now than just a time-piece because it serves as a reminder to "watch" out for those who might walk up to me when I least expect it and say, "What will you give me for this?

I quickly reply, "I don't know. What will you take for it?"

And if he says, "I'll take $15.00 for it."

I reply, "No, I'll give you $10:00."

And SMILE!

Fifty-Cent Piece

<hr />

"I'LL GIVE YOU TWENTY-FIVE CENTS if you will go to church with me tonight," my mother said in a pleading tone of voice.

The church where she attended was having a revival meeting and she wanted me to go, in hopes, of course, that I would "get saved." I knew that no one was going to "save" me. I had plans for my life and they didn't include "getting saved." However, my mother and God had other plans for me.

The fifty-cent piece she offered me was every penny she had in the world, yet she was not going to short change God. She told me to keep a quarter and place the other one in the collection plate when I got to church.

I took Mother up on her offer. I had to walk about a mile down Blaze Branch to the main road where a little "house store" was located. I had planned to get change there at the store, but the church bus arrived early, and I didn't have time to get change for the fifty-cent piece.

I got on the bus firmly clutching the fifty-cent piece inside my trouser pocket. I began to wonder about my dilemma. How was I going to get change for the fifty-cent piece? Then an idea hit me. Why not kept it all? No one would ever know the difference. I contemplated how my plan would work. I would sit at the back of the church because Mother always sat up front where the action was. I would let the plate pass by me and keep the money. No one would ever know except God, and he didn't need the money half as badly as I needed it. It was a perfect plan. At least I though so.

The bus arrived and parked on the side of the road. We had to cross the creek on a small bridge which was located about a quarter of a mile from the little board and batten church building. It sat atop pole stilts backed up against the mountainside. The interior of the church was simple with wooden pews. Banners with various mottoes that meant nothing to me hung everywhere on the wall. The Evangelists preaching the revival were two ladies. One played the accordion, and they sang together.

The music was loud and lively and the people joyfully praised God, except me of course and a few others. We sat back and watched the people clap their hands and dance the Davidic dance of the Old Testament, all to the rhythm of a few guitars, a tambourine or two and the sole accordion the Evangelists had brought with them. I was enjoying listening to the music, especially the guitarist since I was beginning to learn how to play myself. Then I heard the word "offering." I froze.

I thought I was ready for this part of the service, but I was not. Pastor Odus Durham got up and made a plea for a generous offering for the evangelist. I loved him very much and admired his ministry, but I held on to my fifty-cent piece, or should I say my quarter, with all my might. After all, God had a 50% interest in the deal, but I wasn't about to put my money in any offering plate for anyone.

The pastor talked about how people in the Old Testament robbed God of tithes and offerings. I thought he was speaking straight to me. I felt awful. I had God's money and I had to give it back, but I had a serious problem. God's money was tied to my money, and there was no way to separate the two. I reasoned that God would understand if I didn't give His money since it was tied to mine. Surely, God wouldn't expect me to give what was mine if I didn't want to give it. But that didn't work. I literally broke out in a sweat. It was like the showdown at high noon at the O.K. Corral.

The pastor blessed the offering and the usher passed the offering plate down one aisle, and then down another, back and forth until they got to me. I watched them as they got closer and closer to me. I had my hand and arm positioned like a gun fighter ready to draw.

Then it happened. I pulled out the fifty-cent piece and dropped in the plate. After the ushers left I sat there bewildered asking myself, *Why did I give my money a way?* I just figured that it must have been the loud music that dulled my brain and caused me to do such a dumb thing. I was angry. I felt duped. I was never going to attend another church service again as long as I lived. But things got worse.

While I was musing over my loss, the Evangelist got up and preached. I missed most of what she said because I was to upset about what I had done with my money. She talked about sinners giving their lives to God, but I was not interested – not tonight anyway.

After the Evangelist finished her sermon, the pastor gave the invitation. He asked everyone to stand and close their eyes. He emphasized that no one should look around while the invitation was given. Of course, I was in no mood to listen to such nonsense. I was discreet about it, but I raised my head and took a peek. When I did, the pastor and I locked eyes. I felt like a kid caught with his hand in the cookie jar. I dropped my head and closed my eyes and hoped beyond hope that he hadn't seen me. Wrong!

I lowered my head, and then I heard the pastor's footsteps coming down the aisle toward me. They sounded like the gongs of a giant grandfather clock striking midnight. I stood there griping the back of the wooden pew as firmly as I could because I knew he was coming to speak to me. Suddenly the footsteps stopped right where I was, and a gentle hand formed over mine.

He said, "Son, come with me and let's go to the altar and give your life to God."

I didn't say a word. At some point during his plea I shifted my weight from one foot to the other. He thought I was going with him, and when he gave me a little tug on the hand, that was enough to give me the courage to go forward. The dam was broken, and I went to the alter and gave my life to Christ. That night all my unhealed hurt, unmet need and unresolved issues were released to God, and He healed me totally.

On the way home on the church bus I pondered in my heart what God had done for me. It was more than I could fathom. And now after forty-five years serving God as a minister of the Gospel, I still can't understand it all.

Even Me! (John 3:16)

Mel Gibson's wonderful movie entitled "The Passion of The Christ" could not depict the full impact of our Lord's suffering for us sinners. Yet, He did it all out of His amazing grace and wondrous love.

My mother's love gave up her last fifty cents to get me to the revival so I could hear the Word of God and get saved. Only a mother would care so deeply, and I'm glad she did that for me. No amount of money can buy salvation because Jesus paid it all when He died on the Cross. However, discipleship costs a person everything. (Revelations 3:20; Ephesians 2:8-9; I John 1:9)

At any rate, both Mother and I agree that we got our money's worth the night that I coughed up God's fifty-cent piece!

Roy scouted the ridge in the background and passed by the old family cabins in his search for the miracle rabbit. Shown here in front of one where he had lived before are Aunt Mae Potter Hawkins and Easter Potter Cantrell with little James Hawkins on the left.

Almost a Rabbit

IT WAS A COLD DECEMBER DAY, and I awoke with an urge to go rabbit hunting.

I was not your average hunter who depended on conventional methods of hunting such as perseverance and skill. I believed if I couldn't catch a rabbit the old fashioned way, God would short circuit the laws of nature and create a rabbit just for me. At least I though so.

I had seen many miracles growing up under the influence of a godly mother. I witnessed the sick restored to health, flood waters challenged, bleeding stopped, and moonshine turned into water, all through prayer. However, I admit I had never seen a rabbit appear out of nowhere except out of a hat at the circus.

I had only been a Christian about six months and I was anxious to try out my faith wings.

There were no beagles around, so I tried to persuade a couple of old hound dogs that were under the house to join me, but they weren't about to leave their warm beds to chase rabbits in the cold. So I struck out with God and Grandpa's trusty 12 gauge shotgun all by myself. I liked the odds. I'd heard that God and me become a majority.

I made my way to the barn where sometimes rabbits hung out, and then I went up the cow path into the pasture where I could get a good view of the field below. On the way I kicked every clump of brush and waited for a rabbit to run for it, but there was no sign of life of any kind anywhere.

I walked past the old dilapidated log house where we had once lived. Dad had built it for us, and we papered the inside with cardboard boxes from the local Blue and White liquor store. The roof was made from rived (handmade) shingles from white oak trees. Those shingles actually kept the rain out even though I could see stars at night through their sides where they lapped over each other.

I could see the remains of another log cabin directly across the holler. We had lived in it at one time also. It was only a heap of rotten logs now. Just above it was an abandoned coal "bank", an opening in the side of the hill that we had dug out to get our coal for the winter. A lot of memories came back to me, some bad and some good.

I continued up the left ridge around the back of the property and down the right ridge that came to a point overlooking the Potter home place in the valley below. I had walked the entire boundary of the property which consisted of several acres, but no rabbit.

I didn't want to go home empty handed, so I paused and had a serious prayer. I had been praying and expecting to kill a rabbit long before I got to this point, but I thought maybe I needed to bear down a little harder and believe stronger, which I did. In my mediation a Scripture came to me about Abraham in the Bible. When he was in the process of offering up his son Isaac for a sacrifice, God intervened and rescued his son by providing a miraculous ram for the sacrifice.

Now I had it all figured out. I would say to God, "You created a miracle ram for Abraham to sacrifice instead of Isaac.

Therefore, since You are no respecter of persons, You ought to perform a miracle rabbit for me. The only difference would be the size of the miracle, and mine wouldn't be half the trouble since a rabbit's so small.

I stood there motionless viewing the valley below. My mind wandered from place to place. I could see the old Potter home which held many pleasant memories for me. I looked at the old barn where we milked the cows. It was where the livestock stayed on cold days like today, and next to the house was the smoke house where cuts of fresh meat had been salted down earlier for the winter. The final panoramic view yielded no results, so I decided to make my decent into the valley toward the house below.

At some point I paused. At that moment I sensed a rabbit behind me. Don't ask me how I knew it, but I did. I slowly turned my head to the right and when I did it startled a rabbit that had been lying there quietly. The motion should have triggered the rabbit's instinct to escape, but for some unknown reason the rabbit hunkered back down in its hiding position unaware that I had seen it move. He was no more than ten feet away from me. I could have almost hit it with the barrel of my gun. Ordinarily it would have been too close to shoot with a 12 gauge shotgun, but I wasn't about to let this minor problem stop me – not when it was a miracle rabbit that I had prayed for.

To further complicate matters the rabbit was on the wrong side of me to shoot right handed, and it was behind me. I had to place the gun on my left shoulder and shoot left handed which was very awkward, but I managed to slowly turn around and point the gun in the direction of the rabbit and pull the trigger. When the smoke cleared there was just a heap of fur up against the hillside. I went to pick up my miracle rabbit and it was unrecognizable. There wasn't much left of it, but I was determined to make a meal out of what was left anyway.

I arrived at the house with my 12 gauge and a ball of fur in my hand. I laid the "almost rabbit" on the porch bench which held the buckets used for drawing drinking and cooking water from the nearby well, and I went inside to get something to put it in after cleaning it.

When I returned with a bowl, the rabbit had disappeared as quickly as it had appeared on the hillside. Now I had experienced two miracles. The rabbit had appeared and it had disappeared in a matter of a few minutes. Then reality set in when from underneath the house came the sound of hungry dogs growling and fighting over a meal of some kind. It turned out to be my rabbit. The dogs had snatched it from off the water bench while I was inside the house. I was so focused on my miracle rabbit, I had forgotten about the dogs under the floor.

Needless to say I was not a happy hunter. I scolded the dogs, but there was no way to retrieve my miracle rabbit from them. I found myself angry at God for allowing the dogs to spoil a perfectly good miracle. My immaturity demanded an explanation as to why God had answered my prayer by giving me a miracle and then allowing the dogs to take it from me.

Then I heard an inner voice speak to me gently, "Roy, I can make rabbits, and I can take rabbits." That is all I heard, but the message was clear. "It is God who works in you to will and to act according to His good purpose." (Philippians 2:13)

I was glad that God took the initiative and revealed His purpose to me that day. It was certainly better then "almost a rabbit," or a whole rabbit, for that matter.

The Day I Doubted God

———◆———

I REMEMBER THE DAY I DOUBTED GOD like it was only yesterday. I was a senior in High School, and my English teacher, Mrs. Moore, had assigned Frances Greer and me to represent our senior class in the Pike County speech festival to be held at Pikeville College. The speech I was to give was called *The Midnight Ride of Paul Revere* by Henry Wadsworth Longfellow.

I had accepted Christ on May 20, 1958, two days before school was out. I spent part of the summer in youth camp and giving my personal testimony in the area churches. Therefore, I was fired up when I returned to school in the fall. When Mrs. Moore ask me to present a speech, I was delighted for the opportunity, but scared to death to face such a big crowd.

To be sure that I would do a good job, I practiced the speech until I was confident I could give it well. Then the day came to make the trip to Pikeville. We rode the school bus and each one of the students representing their grade were given a couple of dollars to eat lunch. Afterward we were to ride the bus back to school where our regular bus would take us home.

Upon arriving at the college, I was amazed. I had never seen so many people in one place in my life. Panic set in. The very though of speaking in front of so many people and being judged by them was overwhelming. At that moment I felt as Job did when he said, "The thing that I have feared has come upon me." (Job 3:25)

"Fear" is the operative word in Job's statement, and that's what I was experiencing - mortifying fear. I had read Paul's Second Letter to Timothy where he said, "For God hath not given us the spirit of fear; but of power, and of love, and of a sound mind" (II Timothy 1:7). I read it, but I couldn't apply it to myself.

My speech was next. I stood close to Mrs. Moore for assurance, but my stomach was tied in knots. I'm sure she could sense my nervousness because she gave me some encouraging words just before I went on. And then my name was called. I walked out on the stage. Flood lights were shining in my face. It's a wonder that I didn't pass out.

I began with a thunderous … "Listen my children and you shall hear of the midnight ride of Paul Revere, on the eighteenth of April, in seventy-five; hardly a man is now alive who remembers that famous day and year…" I guess it was the word "remember" that got me, because I forgot what to say next. Of course, Mrs. Moore was behind the scene trying to help me, but I lost my hearing at some point. If she had used a bull horn I don't think I could have heard her.

I made it through the speech, but I was totally humiliated. It wasn't just the bad performance, but it was the fact that I had witnessed to all my school mates for the better part of a year and told them how great God was and how He would never let a person down.

Now, I felt God had let me down. And to be honest I never wanted to be a Christian anymore. I refused to ride the bus back home with the other students. I was too embarrassed. I hitch-hiked back home fussing at God all the way, telling Him He had not held up his end of the bargain, and that I wasn't about to stick my neck out anymore for Him.

All weekend I was miserable. I didn't want to return to school but I did. When it came time for Mrs. Moore's English class on Monday afternoon, I went in and put my head down on my desk and wouldn't look up. She called the class to order and proceeded to thank Frances and me for the fine job we did at the speech festival.

Frances received a Superior award for her speech and I received Excellent for mine. I couldn't believe it! I raised my head up, straightened my shoulders and smiled as if I had expected it all the time. What had happened was that I was so humiliated by my performance, I left before I could find out the results. The only award I received when I graduated from High School was the Oratory Award.

I felt very badly that I had doubted God's faithfulness. I repented and apologized to Him for my arrogance and unbelief. But I learned from my mistake. Now when I go through a painful trial I always say to God, "I don't understand what is going on, but I know one thing from past experience. You are faithful, and I trust You to work all things together for my good, no matter what the present situation looks like!" (Romans 8:28)

Grandma's Maytag Miracle

MIRACLES WERE NOT NEW TO ME when I was growing up at home. I saw God work many of them through my godly mother's prayers. I heard her pray one time for God to turn Dad's moonshine into water (See "Moonshine Into Water") and He did. I saw God stop a dog from bleeding to death because Dad decided to cut its ears and tail off on a drunken whim. She prayed and a poisonous snake became harmless. (See "Rattlesnake") She prayed for her family until her alcoholic husband and seven children gave their hearts to God. Miracles at our house were as common as our next breath. However, I had never experienced a miracle through my prayers until the day Grandma's washing machine conked out.

Grandma Potter always washed clothes on the back porch in the summer time. This particular wash day, the machine wouldn't work. It was plugged into a drop socket hanging from the porch ceiling. We examined everything that might cause it to be on the blink. We plugged and unplugged the cord into the socket. We turned the little "on" and "off" switches back and forth but with no success. We checked the fuse box, and it was okay. Then it hit me to pray for it to work. This is what my mother would have done if something didn't work. But I had never prayed for a miracle myself, and I was afraid. What if it didn't work? Then I might doubt God's power from then on.

I finally decided to pray and just see what would happen. So I reached up, grasped the socket and prayed a simple prayer. I flipped the switch and it started washing "…swish…swash, swish…swash, swish…swash!" I was amazed. I think this first miracle got me thinking about praying for bigger ones.

Grandma Potter heard the machine and came out to see why it had started working. She asked, "What happened? How did you fix it?"

I said, "I prayed for it."

She mumbled something under her breath and gathered up some clothes and began to wash them. I believe it prepared the way for me to share the Gospel later with her. I did. The opportunity came one evening when she was building a fire in the wood burner stove to prepare dinner. I wanted to witness to her , but I was scared to death because God was a private matter with everyone I knew except Mother and a few others.

Nevertheless, I mustered up the nerve and asked her bluntly, "Grandma, have you ever repented?"

She was startled and quickly defended herself with the comment, "I want you to know I have not done anything to repent of." Then she paused and said, "I did sin once, but it was necessary." She explained how she had sold moonshine whiskey to pay for the home place. (See "Grandma's Bank") I didn't press the issue.

When it comes to need, I believe we are all similar to Grandma's old Maytag washing machine. We are in dire need of a power surge from outside of ourselves to function. In our case we all are in need of the regenerative power of the Sweet Holy Spirit to bring life to our dead spirits, such as the machine needed a source outside of itself called electricity to work properly.

I shall always believe that God had a higher purpose when he started Grandma's old Maytag that day. It was to jump start the "measure of faith" (Romans 12:3b) placed in her at birth and which resulted in her accepting Christ before she died at the age of 102 years old.

Note: Grandma lived with my mother the last 16 years (1969-1985) of her life. Mother witnessed to her almost daily during that time. What I did was minuscule compared to her. The Apostle Paul said, "I planted, Apollos watered, but God gave the increase." (I Corinthians 3:6)

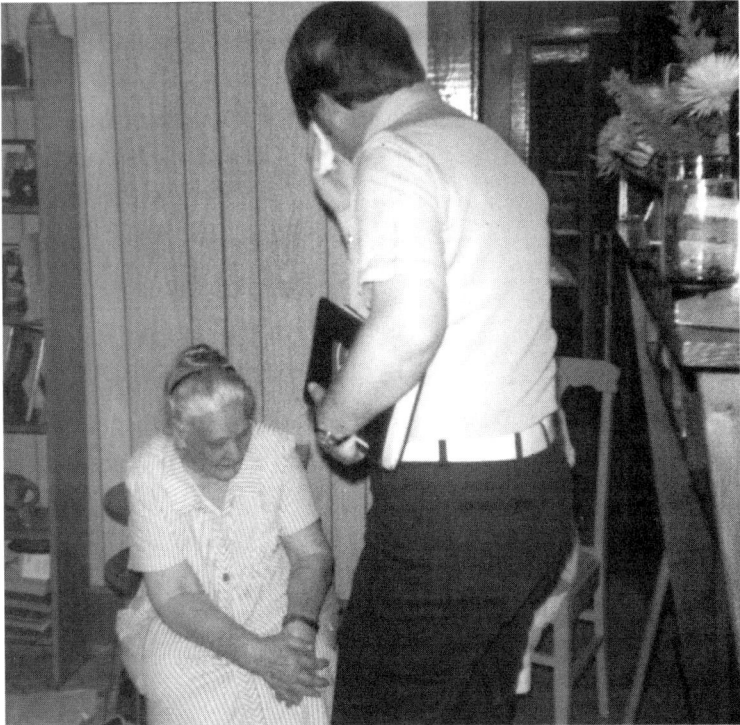

Grandma Potter prays with her grandson, the author.

Ten Cents a Day

IT IS SAID THAT AN APPLE A DAY will keep the doctor away. I found that ten cents a day can keep ignorance away.

I don't remember ever not wanting to learn. I have always had an unquenchable thirst for knowledge. I read in the Bible that one should "study to show thyself approved unto God, a workman that needeth not be ashamed, rightly dividing the word of truth" (II Timothy 2:15). Therefore, when I became a Christian, I wanted to learn everything there was to know about the Bible.

One day while browsing through a Christian magazine I saw an advertisement of a general Bible knowledge correspondence course for $24.00, which was a lot in those days. The cost of the course could be paid for in monthly installments of $2.00 per month. I was receiving twenty-five cents per day for lunch money. So, I devised a plan to pay for the course by saving ten cent per day out of it. With the remaining fifteen cents I bought a Royal Crown Cola and a Moon Pie for lunch.

The course consisted of five booklets and a proctored test for each one. I studied a section and then took the test. I couldn't wait to get the test back in the mail. I had to walk about two or three miles round trip to the post office at Shelby Gap, Kentucky. I would open the envelope very slowly and unfold the test, and when I saw my grade I would rejoice all the way back home. In fact, even as I write this story, I can still feel the excitement of learning that I felt back then.

This is positive proof that God will make a way for anyone to acquire knowledge if he or she is willing to try. I don't believe there is any room for excuses for not doing God's work. The secret is to gain the knowledge for the purpose of furthering God's Kingdom and not for ourselves. Henry Blackaby's book entitled *Experiencing God* put it in perspective when he writes that man's job is to, "find out what God is doing and join Him," not the other way around.

Jesus sometimes asks the impossible of us so that He can show us what He can do with a little if it is placed in His hand. The lad in the Gospel of John, Chapter 6, is one of the best examples of this. The little boy only had two small fish and five barley loaves, but he offered them to Jesus. He fed 5,000 people with the lad's lunch. It is a wonderful story about a lad with a little who was listening and willing to let go of what he had to the glory of God. It is about planting a seed and watching it grow.

I only gave part of my lunch to God, and Jesus took it and blessed it. Not only has He fed me spiritually with the knowledge that I received, but thousands of others also through me. It all started with a desire to study and the sacrifice of a simple dime a day to pay for the knowledge.

I am aware that one cannot put a watermelon into a pea brain, but one can put a whole lot of peas in a watermelon if the watermelon is open and willing to receive. It all depends on whether one is willing to receive knowledge or resist it. The possibilities are limitless. Just as no one knows the number of apples in one apple seed, only eternity can reveal the good that a little can do through one act of obedience. The Bible says, "If you are willing and obedient you shall eat the good of the land." (Isaiah 1:19)

Just ask the lad when you get to heaven. (Read John, Chapter 6.)

Guided By A Dream

WHAT COULD THAT DREAM MEAN? Those were my thoughts as I awoke one morning shortly after I accepted Christ into my heart. It didn't seem spiritual to me at first, but it wouldn't go away. The more I thought about it, the more I was certain that God was trying to tell me something in the dream, so I sought God in prayer.

Previously I had been praying for God's guidance about an invitation that I received from a friend back in West Virginia. We had just moved from there. He wanted me to come and work a few days. I desperately needed the money to buy some clothes for my senior year of High School. The problem was my father did not want me to go. He had just moved the family back to Kentucky because the mines in West Virginia had shut down, and he was out of work. I had been staying with my grandparents up until then, but moved back in with my family when they returned to Kentucky.

Things were still tense at home because of the problems Dad and I had over the shot gun shells and burned school books. (See "Tree House" and "The Fire That Would Not Go Out")

God knew that I needed a release through divine intervention or I would not go. I was eighteen years old, but I still honored my father. In fact, not long afterward Dad sold my dog (See "Ole Rowdy"), and I accepted my father's authority.

I was desperate to know God's will about the trip. So I believe that God gave me this dream to let me know it was alright to go back to West Virginia and work and earn money for some clothes for school.

Here is what I dreamed. I was in a used furniture store, and I was there to purchase furniture. I was browsing through the store checking the prices. There were poster board signs either sitting on the furniture or attached to the back advertising the price.

When I awoke, all I could think of was three of the numbers that I saw on the furniture. The numbers were: 6-1-10. I had no clue what they meant. Then, the revelation came from the Holy Spirit. The numbers had to do with the Bible somehow. I had not read the Bible much up until then, but I just knew God had a message for me in there, and it had to do with these three numbers.

I began to search in the Bible for an answer. I took the numbers and went back and forth trying to find something that made sense to me. Then, it happened. I turned to the sixth book of the New Testament, the first chapter and the tenth verse. It said, "Making request, if by any means now at length I might have a prosperous journey by the will of God to come unto you." (Romans 1:10). I knew immediately that God had given me permission to go, and I did.

I had no money to go on a bus, so I hitched the 120 miles back to Newhall, West Virginia, and worked for three days. I also gave my testimony of how God had saved me and called me to preach. It was a wonderful "prosperous" trip.

On my return I stopped in Bradshaw, West Virginia, and bought enough clothes for school — two shirts, two pairs of blue jeans, some socks and underclothes and a black bow tie to wear to church. I alternated the two outfits by washing one out each night for the next day of school, and they lasted me the entire year.

I have learned a lot about the Bible since God revealed His will to me in this dream years ago. One thing is that the Bible is full of instances where God spoke to people in dreams. In fact, when we are asleep it is the one time that God can speak to us. Someone said that there is no atheist when they are asleep because God has access to every man's spirit then.

You don't have to be a saint for God to access your dreams. Pharaoh in the Bible is a good example. He was the ruler of Egypt at the time Joseph the son Jacob was sold into slavery by his brothers and carried to Egypt to become Pharaoh's slave. Pharaoh dreamed two dreams. He became very troubled and couldn't sleep. He wanted to know the meaning of these dreams. He called for his wise men (soothsayers), but they couldn't tell him the meaning. Joseph, by the power and providence of God, interpreted Pharaoh's dreams, and was promoted to second in command. (Genesis 41:31-44)

I believe God uses us today even as he died Joseph in dreams and visions. Ezekiel, Daniel Peter, John and others in the Bible dreamed and saw visions. This is prophesied in Joel 2:28-29.

I have had other dreams that were even more phenomenal than this one, but they were few and far between. I don't exalt dreams above God's Word, because all dreams are not from God. They can be the result of too much to eat at night. But God can and does speak through dreams, and when He does you will know it.

I like the line in Rudyard Kipling's poem "IF": "If you can dream and not make dreams yours master... then you'll be a man, my son."

Guitar Miracle

I BELIEVE MOST BOYS AND GIRLS who are born in Appalachia have a fondness for music and dream at one time or other of singing and playing the guitar, banjo or fiddle. It was certainly my dream to play like some of the greats of my day such as Chet Adkins or Lester Flat and Earl Scruggs.

It is one thing to desire to play music, and it is an entirely different thing to actually have the skill to play. To have music in one's blood is helpful in getting started, but to become a skilled musician it takes time, practice and patience. On the other hand, there is a component in music more important than skill and that is talent. Still sometimes there is an outright miracle gift that comes from God, and it can come instantly as the result of prayer. The latter is what happened to me.

Although I loved stringed instruments and tried to play them, I could not. I sought out musicians for assistance, but they couldn't help me. I knew if I played an instrument, it would take divine intervention, which it did.

I believe that if a person desires to play musical instruments, he or she should practice. It is appropriate to pray when you practice. But I also believe that God will endow a person with special abilities beyond a person's capability when he or she desires the gift to glorify God. I don't believe God will gift a lazy person. In my case I practiced but couldn't play, so I asked God to help me, and he did.

Late one evening I was walking home from a revival meeting strumming a guitar hung around my neck. It was a sweet little Martin guitar loaned to me by a lady in town. It didn't have a regular strap, just a string, but it worked okay. I was just learning to play a few chords, mostly G-C-D.

My heart's desire was to pick the guitar like Chet Adkins. His style is unique. He uses his thumb to keep rhythm with a "thump...thump...thump" sound while at the same time picking out the melody with his fingers. The design is somewhat like patting your head and rubbing your stomach and chewing gum at the same time.

That evening as I walked through the little town of Neon, Kentucky, strumming on the guitar, I realized that I was playing the Chet Adkins style. It was something I could not do before. I played until late in the night, paused only momentarily to rest, and then I played some more for fear that I would lose it.

When I awoke the next morning I grabbed the guitar and found that I could still play. I've been playing ever since. The same thing happened to me with the banjo. One minute I couldn't play, and the next minute I could in spite of trying my best to play it on my own. There is no way to explain what happened in each case except you would have to agree that both were miracles from God.

When I read this story to our son, Howie, over the telephone, he told me something that happened to him recently. He said that he was eating alone at a restaurant just before going to class, when a father and his six-year-old daughter came in and were seated next to him. The little girl was vibrant and she flipped around like a little butterfly all excited about having dinner with her father. She told her father that she had one dollar but needed five more to go with it for a special event at school. She had no lack of enthusiasm to ask her father for exactly what she needed. And he had no lack of eagerness to grant her request.

Don't you see? We all have a "measure of faith" but we don't have everything. Our Heavenly Father takes up the slack, but we must ask him for what we need. The little girl knew that her father would meet her every need, and he did. He took great pleasure in providing the five dollars. The key is not found in the need as much as in the fact that the need brought the two of them closer together.

Our Heavenly Father knows what we need before we ask, but He wants us to ask Him for it. He too takes great pleasure in "supplying all of our needs according to his riches in glory by Jesus Christ." (Philippians 4:19) It is not just for need's sake but for relationship's sake.

Jesus said, "Ask and it shall be given you; seek, and ye shall find; knock, and it shall be opened unto you." (Matthew 7:7) He went on to say "For everyone that asketh receiveth, and he that seeketh findeth, and to him that knocketh it shall be opened." (Matthew 7:8)

If you take the first letter of "**a**sk, **s**eek and **k**nock," they spell the word **ASK**. The Bible says that God is no respecter of persons. He loves to give gifts to his children and to fulfill the very desires of the heart, as we delight in Him (Psalm 37:4)

What is your burning need right now? Why don't you "ASK" Jesus for it just like the little girl did in this story? It's not about music or money or anything else. It's all about RELATIONSHIP! When you ask it will be music in our Heavenly Father's ears.

Evangelists Roy Cantrell and Reed North at a revival in Paris, Tennessee in 1961. Roy is playing the guitar.

Roy and his friend, Reed North, served as evangelists together following Roy's first overwhelming trip to the city of Chattanooga.

The Lights Of Chattanooga

$$\Longrightarrow\!\!\!\!\diamond\!\!\!\!\Longleftarrow$$

"THE LIGHTS OF BROADWAY" could not have shown any brighter than did the lights of Chattanooga, Tennessee, the night I came into town across Missionary Ridge riding in a Greyhound bus. It was a breathtaking sight for an 18 year old boy right out of the hills of eastern Kentucky. I had never seen anything thing like it in my life. And to this day, when I see those lights at night, whether it is from Lookout Mountain, Signal Mountain or Missionary Ridge, I still get a thrill.

The purpose of my trip to Chattanooga was to stay with Pastor Donald Hall and go to Bible school in Cleveland, Tennessee, and to conduct a revival at his church in Orange Grove. After the two week revival, I returned home via the same Greyhound bus with no thought of ever returning. I had a hard time adjusting to city life.

When I arrived in Chattanooga, I was so naive that I didn't even know what a pizza was. I had never seen or eaten one before. I had heard the expression "pizza pie" so I though pizzas were sweet like a regular pie. When the pastor told me that we would have pizza as a going away meal, I made the comment that I didn't like to eat anything sweet before I traveled because sweets made me sick. The pastor explained to me that pizzas weren't sweet.

The night I was to leave for Kentucky, the pastor's family and a friend of mine from Cleveland took me to a pizza place in town. I ordered a sausage pizza to be on the safe side. When it came I kept waiting to eat it, and the pastor asked me why I wasn't eating my pizza. I told him that I was waiting for my sausage.

He said, "The sausage is on your pizza."

I was embarrassed because I was expecting sausage patties. After this incident, I decided the city was no place for me, and I would stay in the mountains of Kentucky and preach. I soon found God had other plans for me, and they included Chattanooga.

My life is a true testimony to the fact that God can use anyone, no matter their background and lack of ability. The Bible says that God has chosen the "foolish things" to confound the wise. (I Corinthians 1:27) This doesn't mean that He chooses stupid people because He likes to major on stupidity. It reflects how God chooses the most "unlikely vessel" to put His life into, and the results will not be by man's might, but by the manifestation of the power of God. This gives everyone hope to know that God can and does use frail, imperfect people to accomplish His purposes.

God brought me back to Chattanooga almost thirty years later to pastor a church. I didn't make the choice, God did! And every time I go across Missionary Ridge at night, I remember how those lights impacted my life. I was just a teenager then, and now I am a senior citizen. Then I just saw lights, but now I see the lights as souls. Then, I was just passing through, but now I have become one of the lights of our fair city. It is my prayer that I too shall shine brightly and inspire another soul who might be just passing in the night, as I did, and be blessed by the Lights of Chattanooga.

A letter To God

ONE MEMORIAL DAY IN 1963, I decided to write God a letter. I had received my call into the ministry and though I wanted Bible training, I knew I couldn't afford to go to seminary. My desire was to attend Moody Bible Institute.

I was married then, and we were expecting our first child. We barely had enough money to live on. I didn't know anyone who could bail me out, but I knew my Father owned the cattle on a thousand hills, and, even though it may sound strange, I decided to sit down and make my request known to Him and ask for His help.

I poured out my heart to God on plain notebook paper. Like a child writing a note to his best friend, I told God how much I loved him and how badly I wanted to go to Moody Bible Institute. It felt wonderful to unload my care about my need for an education on someone who would listen to me and someone who really cared and could help me. The letter was my way of making a tangible contact with God. I just knew that He was going to answer my plea. I just knew it! I finished the letter and sealed it with the words "sealed in the name of the Father and the Son and the Holy Spirit…. Not to be opened until answered."

By faith, I filled out an application and sent it to the registrar's office at Moody. They wrote back to say they were considering my application but that I needed to come to Chicago so that they could interview me personally. There was no guarantee that I would be accepted. Our son was due in March, and we needed every penny for the delivery, so I couldn't go.

About two year later, out of the clear blue, my denomination appointed me to a small church on the northwest side of Chicago. I never asked for the appointment. No one except my wife and God knew about my desire to attend Moody. After we were settled in our apartment in Cicero, a suburb on the southwest of the city, I went to Moody and talked to the registrar. I was permitted to enroll as a "special student" which was the same status as for missionaries.

Some of the best Bible training I have received was at Moody. After forty years, I still remember teachers who touched my life and taught me the Word of God that has kept me a balanced preacher.

One day after I had enrolled at Moody, I was looking through my desk, and I found the letter I had written God years before, still sealed. I opened it and cried tears of joy at the faithfulness of God.

Sometimes the simplest thing gets God's attention. Like the child who gave his lunch of two fish and five small barley loaves to Jesus. Jesus didn't reject the childish faith but embraced it, feeding over 5000 people with the lad's offering.

I'm also reminded of the story of the Shunamite woman who sought healing for her daughter. (Matthew 15) How trusting and persistent she was in her request, stating, "Even the dogs get the crumbs from the Master's table." Jesus commented that

He had never seen such faith not even in Israel (Matthew 15:28), "and her daughter was made whole from that very hour."

God is faithful. He loves us and wants a relationship with us even if it as simple as writing Him a letter. I marvel at how willing God is to connect with us by whatever means He can. God received my letter, and He read it, and He answered it. He gave me the desire of my heart. (Psalm 10:17) All I did was humble my heart as a child and pour it out to God in simple faith. That simple act of faith moved Him to answer my prayer. Isn't that what the Bible says;? "Call unto me and I will answer thee and show you great and mighty things." (Jeremiah 33:3)

I can just imagine my letter arriving in The Almighty's presence, having ridden on the wings of the sweet Holy Spirit without the help of any earthly Postal Service, stamped with bright red letters that read: "Special delivery…. Handle with care!"

Reflection

HAVE YOU EVER BEEN SO COLD you felt you knew what the expression "freeze to death" meant? This is how I felt on that blustery day in December. I was standing inside Tucker's Restaurant in Neon, Kentucky, admiring my brand new Volkswagen Rabbit parked directly in front of the establishment. Snow had just begun to fall.

My attention was drawn to what appeared to be a homeless man standing outside in the cold. He was also admiring my new car and was huddled up against the glass of the restaurant window to get away from the piercing wind. He appeared to be between twenty-five and thirty years old but looked much older. He had long matted hair and a shaggy beard. His clothes looked as if they had been slept in, and his bare toes were protruding out of the holes in his tennis shoes.

Mother was back at the cash register talking to someone she knew. It was customary for Mother and me to go to town twice a year when I came home around July and between Christmas and New Years. When I came home, the first thing Mother did was take me to Dawahare's and Sam Hush's clothing store to shop for me a suit or a pair of shoes. Then we would stop at the restaurant for a sandwich and just talk.

As I watched the man admire my new car, I felt guilty that I had a new car and this man didn't have anything. I was about to go outside and offer him something to eat or some money when he suddenly turned and looked straight into my face. I couldn't believe my eyes. He was my brother, Auldin! That moment shall forever be etched in my memory.

Of the eight children in our family of four boys and four girls, Auldin has always been the center of affection. He is smart, gifted and fun. Kaye, my wife, tells him all the time that he is the best one of all the boys. I think she means it.

Auldin's life story is not a pretty one. He became addicted to drugs and alcohol at a very young age, and they almost destroyed his life. In fact, if it had not been for a praying mother, he would be dead today. He and I enrolled in college the same year. He wanted to be an artist and he could have been a good one, but drugs got the best of him. He has probably been incarcerated more times than anyone else in his home town, or county, for that matter. He came close to death many times. Satan wanted Auldin dead, but prayer kept him alive.

Auldin told me of a time when God spared his life. He said his best friend, who was also a druggie, invited him to go hunting one day. Auldin had a 410 gauge shotgun, and his friend had a twelve gauge. Auldin was banging on a hollow tree to scare a squirrel out, and when he turned around his friend was aiming his shotgun at him. His friend looked scared!

Auldin asked him what was wrong, and he said, "I saw God."

Two years passed before he saw him again and while they were sitting at the table, the friend said, "Auldin, do you remember when we went hunting that day?"

Auldin said, "Yes."

"Well, I took you up there in the woods to kill you."

Auldin replied, "For what reason?"

The man said, "I though you were coming on to my wife."

Auldin said that he got angry and asked, "Then why didn't you do it?"

His friend replied, "An angel came down above you and said 'You can't do that.'"

The next day Auldin received word that his friend was dead. He had OD'ed on alcohol and drugs that same night.

After his friend died, Auldin almost died himself in a car accident. He and a couple of his friends were out doing drugs and drinking one afternoon when the driver lost control of his car and it slammed into the embankment on the other side of a creek. The estimated speed according to the police report was in excess of 120 mph.

The E.M.T'S report on Auldin read, "No respiration; no heartbeat; no eye dilation…. response: Deceased."

The policeman who arrived on the scene knew Auldin and took him up in his arms and said, "Take him to the hospital."

The medical team air lifted him in a helicopter to the University Hospital intensive care unit in Lexington, Kentucky. On the way to the hospital they resuscitated him. He sustained a fractured skull, brain injury, both jaws broken, dislocated shoulder, crushed wrist and knee, and lower back injuries. The report shows that the medical teams lost him twice on the way to Lexington in the helicopter.

The first words that came out of Auldin's mouth when he awoke from a coma were, "I am going toward the light." Auldin told me that demons were trying to get him into the lake of fire.

He said they were little short gross demons with big eyes. He likened them to the demons in the movie of the *Passion of the Christ* by Mel Gibson.

They tried to throw him into the lava, but they weren't strong enough. He also recognized friends of his who had died. They had on beach towels, enticing him to come into the lava as if it weren't bad. He refused.

Then a strong spirit came who had no appearance but who had power and began to put him into the fire. About that time Jesus came walking down a corridor toward Auldin. When Jesus got to the evil spirit, Jesus said something to him, and the evil spirit turned his back to Jesus and bowed over in submission. Then, Jesus nodded his head for Auldin to follow him. As he followed Jesus, he saw the light that most people claim to see when they have a near death experience. This vision changed Auldin's life.

Shortly after this harrowing experience, he gave his heart to the Lord, and now he is living in Cleveland, and I am his pastor. He serves as an usher, writes songs and sings. He is a wonderful blessing to everyone who knows him. Now I can say not only is Auldin my blood brother, but he is also my brother in Christ. We are now double brothers.

A lot has changed in Auldin's life since the day he stood outside Tucker's Restaurant in Neon, Kentucky. Then he was a drug addict; now he is a Jesus addict. Then he was headed for hell; now he is headed for heaven. Then he was clothed in filthy rags; now he is clothed in the righteousness of God. Then he was a child of the devil, and now he is a child of the King.

To me the pane of glass at the restaurant symbolizes the separation of light and darkness. On one side is the blessed

Grace of God, and on the other side is the curse of sin. On one side is God's mercy, and on the other side is God's justice. On one side is God love, joy and peace, and on the other side are hatred, sadness and chaos. On one side is the promise of eternal life, and on the other side is eternal damnation.

God taught me a lesson in humility the day Auldin turned around and we faced each other through the restaurant window. The lesson is: every lost soul is a reflection of every child of God, except for the grace of God!

The Cantrell children: Kate, Dora, Zetta, the author Roy, and Novella, with their father holding Auldin on his knee. Little Junior, who followed Novella in age, died at 3 1/2. Michael, the eighth child, had not yet been born. Their mother, Easter, took the photograph. They were living at Newhall, (Second Bottom coal camp) West Virginia.

"Can You Hear Me Now?"

THERE IS A COMMERCIAL ON TELEVISION in which a certain phone company demonstrates how their phone network reaches everywhere. To prove their point they send a man all over with a cell phone up to his ear repeating the phrase: "Can you hear me now?"

One day God got my attention about my prejudice against Catholics, but I refused to answer, so God kept calling until I heard him loud and clear. God's used a crises in my life to get my attention.

One evening I was rushed to the hospital in an ambulance because of a serious loss of blood as the result of a nose bleed. A vein broke in my nasal cavity and the only way to repair it was to have surgery or to pack my nostril with 40 feet of gauze covered with Vaseline. The doctors chose the later procedure. Also, I was given six pints of blood and put on heavy doses of morphine for pain. I almost died. (See "Black Tunnel and Bright Light")

I spent six days in the hospital, and each time I awoke, I saw a Nun standing over me praying. She was always there by my bedside, softly whispering prayers for me. The image of her standing over me praying and making the sign of the Cross, will always be etched in my memory. I don't recall what she looked like, nor do I remember her name, but I shall always be grateful to God for sending me a angel in the form of an "anonymous Nun" to pray for me. Believe me when one is dying there is no room for prejudice.

Sometimes I think God has a real sense of humor because when I recovered from my sickness, He sent me to pastor a church in Morgan City, Louisiana, where the populace must have been eighty per cent Catholic. It was as if God was saying, "O.K., Roy, I have given you the lecture, and now for the test!"

The test was open book. I spent two years in Louisiana ministering alongside Catholics. Then I moved to Cleveland, Tennessee, and enrolled in college. It was there that God opened another door to teach me even more about His love and grace toward all of His children.

One day while I was in college I picked up a Christian magazine and saw where students at Loyola University, a Catholic University in New Orleans, were having an outpouring of the Holy Spirit. I felt impressed to call the Chaplain at Loyola, Reverend Harold Cohen, and ask him if our Chorale could come to their campus and join them in a celebration service. He readily agreed and offered our students and faculty accommodations in the homes of their parishioners.

Our visit to Loyola University was splendid. The first night the Student Center was filled with several hundred spirit filled students and faculty. The President attended for the first time. The praise and worship was extra special. The praise came in waves beginning at the back of the room and moving toward the front and then back again like the waves on an ocean beach.

The next day, the local parishioners took the Chorale to visit The Church of The Most Holy Name of Jesus located on campus. We were admiring the beautiful paintings, sculptures, and architecture when one of the parishioners said with a sweep of the hand, "All of this is beautiful, but it means nothing to us compared to Jesus." His statement put it all in perspective.

Before we left Tennessee for Louisiana, the wonderful people at the church where we pastored for two years invited us to participated in a joint Protestant-Catholic celebration of praise and worship at the Holy Cross Catholic Church in Morgan City. I was thrilled. This is when I met Sister Cor Marie who was our hostess and welcomed us upon our arrival.

We encountered a problem the very first thing; there were no electric outlets in the church to plug in the sound equipment. The community had been invited and they were beginning to gather at the church. I panicked, but Sister Cor Marie remained calm. Now this is where things get interesting.

Sister Cor Marie coolly suggested that we walk next door and get some extension cords to hook up the equipment. So she and I exited the church under a covered sidewalk which was lined with flowers on both sides. The lights under the canopy came on. They were triggered by the approach of nightfall.

We were walking along not saying a word when suddenly Sister Cor Marie held out her arm in front of me and whispered, "Stop!" I froze. I didn't have a clue as to what was going on until I saw a tiny little humming bird drinking nectar from the flowers.

I don't know how long we stood there watching, but, as I stood still with only the flutter of the humming bird's wings breaking the silence, I could almost hear a still small voice say to me, "This is God.... Can you hear me now?" By the time the little humming bird flew away, I was totally relaxed. Then, Sister Cor Marie made a statement that I have never forgotten, She said, "I never fail to take time to observe God's handiwork."

Sister Cor Marie's peace in a crises and her appreciation for God's tiniest little bird caused me to realize that she had a relationship with our Creator that I did not have.

I never saw Sister Cor Marie again after that night, nor do I remember the name of the little "anonymous" Nun in Chicago who faithfully prayed for me, but there is no doubt in my mind but that one day I will see both of them in heaven. I can't wait to give them both a great big hug and thank them for letting God use them to love the prejudice out of me. Yes, God, I can hear you now!

Black Tunnel and Bright Light

TUNNELS ARE SCARY TO ME. Maybe it is because my sister Kate and I were forced to go through one in West Virginia at night without a flashlight to buy moonshine for our dad when he got drunk. We would be horrified when we were awakened in the middle of the night and told we had to go about a mile to the next coal camp to get it. We had to go through the tunnel because it was a short cut. Otherwise, we would have had to walk about three miles one way to get there.

One of the reasons I hated to go through the tunnel was because it was rumored that a man had gotten run over by the train that ran through carrying coal to the big cities. Also, it was said that kidnappers waited for children in the "man holes" located on both sides of the tunnel walls. A "man hole" was a place made in the wall of the tunnel so that a person could stand in it until the train passed through.

When we went through the tunnel, Kate would hold to my clothes, and I would place one hand against the wall and feel my way along. I dreaded the moment when my hand fell into the "man hole" because I just knew a man would be lurking in there to grab us.

If the train came while you were in there, the smoke could suffocate you. It was a scary place. The trains were coal burning, and smoke would fill the tunnel to where you couldn't breathe. If you survived the smoke, you had to reach one of the "man holes" to escape from getting hit by the train. Our hearts would race if we heard the slightest sound that might indicate that the train was coming.

The tunnel was about 100 yards long and curved in the shape of a macaroni. Once our eyes became acclimated to the pitch darkness of the tunnel, the slightest bit of light coming from the other end indicated to us that we were half way through it, and we would breathe a sigh of relief.

After Dad died, Mother and all of us children went back to West Virginia. We visited friends and went to places we had lived. The old tunnel was what Kate and I wanted to see. It was the same except trains didn't run through it much anymore because the coal mines were worked out. Michael, the baby of our clan, picked up a large rock from the tunnel entrance as a souvenir for me, and I still have it.

Many years later I had a near death experience. My problem started with a simple nosebleed. In a short period of time, I lost a great deal of blood. When the elders from the church came and prayed for me, the blood would stop, but soon as they left, it would start again. I kept getting weaker. Finally, my wife insisted that I go to the doctor and called an ambulance. I vaguely recall going. I had almost waited too late, and I had to be hospitalized.

During the dying process I went into a tunnel. I knew I was dying, but I wasn't afraid. I said to myself, "I am going to see how it is when a person dies." The dying process started with me flying like Superman with my arms extended in front of me through a dark tunnel. I was weightless and moved slowly toward a brilliant bright light that was far away at first but got even brighter as I flew closer to it.

This tunnel I was flying through was round and the sides were very black and wavy, something like a metal corrugated drain used under roadways. As I was flying toward the light, at some point my momentum slowed to a stop, but I didn't fall. For a moment I remained suspended in mid air weightless. Then, I began to slowly exit the tunnel feet first and was reunited with my body.

After I was released from the hospital, I called my doctor to ask him if I could drive my car.

He said, "Reverend, no, you cannot drive your car. You almost died. You were knocking on the door." I realized then that what I experienced was real and not a hallucination.

The lesson from these two tunnel experiences removes all fear of the sting of death.

The literal tunnel — the one my sister and I went through in West Virginia — represents life as we know it, and it can be horrifying at times. The "heavenly" tunnel I experienced the night when I almost died was peaceful and painless and is a pathway to life eternal.

Since this encounter I have heard of others who have gone through similar experiences. All of them speak of a tunnel and being drawn toward a bright light. Surprisingly, all of them who came back did not want to leave the presence of the light and return to earth. This should bring encouragement to realize that Jesus, the Light of the world, stands at the other end of the tunnel to welcome us with open arms and with the greeting:

"My child, well done. You have been faithful over a few things, I will make you ruler over many things. Enter into the joys of the Lord." (Matthew 25:23)

Praise God!

The tunnel in Newhall, West Virginia, that terrified Roy and Kate on night errands to get moonshine for their father.

Gabriel

CHRISTMAS EVE HAS ALWAYS BEEN an exciting time for me. Especially the one when Jack Wright and I picked up a hitchhiker whom we believed to be an angel sent from God. Here's what happened. You be the judge.

Jack and I were very close and actually began our ministry at the same time. Several years later we became family. My mother-in-law married his father after the death of their spouses. As a family we were celebrating Christmas together. Even though we had remained in close contact over the years, this particular year was special due to the marriage

We had opened presents earlier at my house, Jack and I decided to drive across town and visit his dad and my mother-in-law for a few minutes. It was getting late so after a short visit, we decided to go back over to my house to spend the night. I was driving my old red, white and blue Chevrolet pick-up truck whose previous owner operated an Exxon gas station. I remember commenting on how cold it was that night.

After we had traveled about one mile we came to an intersection and were about to turn left onto Lee Highway when we noticed a man straight in front of my headlights standing beside the road hitchhiking. He did not have a winter coat on. He was wearing a white summer "Florida/Caribbean" type suit. We pulled over and he climbed into the truck with us.

We told him where we were going, and to our surprise he said that he was headed in the same direction. We introduced ourselves. He said he was from the Middle East. His complexion was an olive nature, but he did not speak with an accent. When we arrived at his destination, he thanked us for the ride and made the comment that the people in Cleveland were not as friendly as they once were. The place we let him out of the truck was very close to the church parsonage where I lived.

After he got out, I turned into the next driveway to my left, stopped, put the truck in reverse and backed into the street to go back the way we came. It only took a few seconds to turn around. I was expecting to see the man walking toward the house, but the man had disappeared. He had vanished in an instant!

It was impossible for him to get to the house by the time we turned around. I have actually gone back to the location several times just to judge the distance to see if it were possible for a person to get to the house in question in that space of time. There was no way for that to happen, not even if he ran.

Jack and I both looked at each and said in one voice, "Where did he go?"

There was a moment of silence, and then Jack said, "Roy, do you remember what the man's name was?"

I hesitated for a moment and then it dawned on me. "Yes, his name was Gabriel"

Then the reality set in that we had given a ride to an angel. We had been in the presence of an angel on Christmas

Eve. What joy filled our hearts! We recalled the Scripture that said, "Beware who you entertain because you may entertain an Angel unaware." (Hebrews 13:2)

We shouted and praised God because we felt for a moment that we had been in the presence of one of the angels who had made that first announcement of the birth of Christ on that first Christmas Eve and who said, "For unto you is born this day in the city of David a Savior who is Christ the Lord. And suddenly there was with the angel a multitude of the heavenly host praising God, and saying, 'Glory to God in the highest, and on earth peace, good will toward men.'" (Luke 2:11,13,14)

A few months later, I received a called from a college professor in town who informed me that a man was dying of cancer and that he requested that I come to his house and pray for him. When I arrived at the address I was given, I was surprised to find that it was the same location where Jack and I had taken Gabriel that Christmas Eve.

It even gets stranger because when I introduced myself and told the family my purpose for being there, no one knew anything about the call, and certainly the sick man was not able to make it. However, the family was cordial and seemed glad that I came. They ushered me into where the sick man was lying in bed. He was lucid but very sick. He did not know me, nor had I ever seen him before that day. I shared Christ with him. We prayed together and I left. I never thought about asking the family if they knew anyone by the name of Gabriel. In all likelihood they didn't.

As I walked down the driveway toward my car, my mind was in a whirl. I kept thinking about the night Jack and I dropped

Gabriel off in that exact spot on Christmas Eve. I felt the man I had just prayed for and Gabriel were connected somehow, but I couldn't prove it to others.

As for Jack and me, no one will ever be able to convince us otherwise!

My Name Is Darwin

⋙◆⋘

IT WAS A MONDAY MORNING and my day off from the office but not from heaven's schedule. I was soon to discover that God had planned a divine encounter with a man named Darwin.

This morning was no different from most others. When I awake each day I say, "This is a Good News day!" Why? "Because this is the day that the Lord has made, and I will rejoice and be glad in it."

Next, I ask the Lord to lead me to a person that needs help whether saved or unsaved. He often does just that. This was one of those days that God heard my prayer and brought me in contact with a man who desperately needed God's help.

I was cruising up Interstate 75 in my antique Lincoln Town Car behind an 18-wheeler. I was feeling good, minding my own business, when suddenly, one of the rear tires of the semi truck that I was following exploded. A huge piece of tread came off and hit my car, and I ran over it. The driver immediately slowed down and turned on his emergency blinkers. The next exit was only about a mile away. I figured that he would get off there to repair the tire, so I got off with him to check my damage.

He pulled off the exit and drove into a truck stop. I followed behind and waited for him to exit his truck. I knew that he was aware I might have damage to my vehicle and that I was behind him in my car. He finally got out of his truck and came back to examine the flat tire.

I exited my car and looked it over. Except for a huge black mark made by the tire on my bumper, there was no visible damage done to the exterior. I didn't know what damage might have been done to the undercarriage, so I walked back to where the driver of the truck was checking his tire.

I introduced myself. He said that his name was Darwin and that he had seen what had happened. He had tried to contact his company via computer but had not been successful. He said that he would try again. He climbed up into the cab of the truck and proceeded to manipulate the computer keys in an effort to report the accident. He tried over and over but couldn't get through.

I had never been around 18-wheelers much, and I was surprised at how high the cab was from the ground. I stood there looking up at Darwin while he worked the computer. Then it hit me! The accident was not about his tire or my car. This was about a "divine appointment." God had orchestrated the whole event. Darwin had a need, and God had sent me to help him. What other explanation could there be?

Let me say right here that I praise God for Dr. D. James Kennedy, the president and founder of Evangelism Explosion (E.E.) and pastor of Coral Ridge Presbyterian Church, Ft. Lauderdale, Florida, for training me in E.E. Dr. Kennedy has been a friend and colleague of mine for the past twenty-five years. Evangelism Explosion is one of the best methods of equipping people to share the Gospel with others. The training I received in E.E. made it possible for me to lead this man to Christ.

I asked Darwin if I could pose a question to him. He consented. "Darwin," I said, "Do you know for sure that if you were to die today you would go to heaven?"

"No" he replied, "I would split hell wide open." Those were his exact words.

I asked him why he believed that.

He told me his story. "Just before I left on this trip my wife informed me that she wanted a divorce. We have been married for twelve years, and we have two beautiful daughters. I was devastated. Last night, I stayed in a motel and I read the Bible that was in the room hoping to get an answer." (Thank God for the Gideon ministry. I have supported it for years. It is a worthy cause.)

He continued, "I found a verse that said 'Call on me and I will answer you.' I was desperate, so I got down on my knees and said, 'God, If this Bible is true and You exist, please answer my prayer and give me a sign that You hear me.' I prayed, but God did not answered my prayer."

I looked up at him sitting there frantically punching computer keys trying to contact his company to report the accident. I said, "Darwin, shut the computer off and let's talk because I don't want you to report this accident. I don't believe there is any damage to my car. This has happened because of your prayer. Why do you think I am here talking to you? God did hear your prayer, and He sent me to let you know that He does exist and that He loves you." I continued: "You have someone praying for you. Who is it?"

"It is my mother," he replied and began to cry.

I said, "Darwin, God has heard your mother's prayers and your prayer and He wants to give you the gift of eternal life. "Then, I asked him if he would like to receive the gift of eternal life."

He began to sob. Tears flowed from his eyes dropping onto his trousers and splattering on the running board of the truck. He replied, "Yes, I would."

I shared the gospel with him, and right there sitting in the cab of his semi truck, Darwin received Christ into his life. I gave him some scriptures to read, and I prayed for him and his wife to be reconciled. The last time I saw Darwin, he was still on his computer trying to get through to his earthly headquarters to report his flat tire, but apparently the line was still busy. I was glad that God's line is never too busy for us to get through to Him when we are in trouble.

Darwin's name has always stuck with me since the day we met. One reason is that our meeting was a divine appointment beyond a shadow of doubt. And not only that, but just a few miles from where Darwin was glorious saved, the infamous "Scopes Monkey Trial" (Creation vs. Evolution) was held in Dayton, Tennessee, in 1925. How could I forget that name? I wished that Sir Charles Darwin, the English naturalist who believed that people evolved from primitive monkeys, could have been present to witness Darwin's birth into the Kingdom of God — something that a monkey could never experience no matter how much he evolves.

The Day Dad Got It!

SOME PEOPLE CALL IT *DEJA VIEU*. Opra Winfry calls it "a light bulb moment." I call it revelation of the Holy Spirit.

The mountain people of my dad's generation struggled a great deal with legalism. They didn't trust anyone outside of the hills, not even preachers and sometimes for good reason. Most of the people in the early history of Appalachia were uneducated, and outsiders took advantage of their illiteracy — especially the coal companies who duped them out of their mineral and timber rights. Then, after the companies mined the coal, they left the environment in a mess and the people to eke out a living the best they could from contaminated fields and fish from polluted streams.

Striped of everything but their pride, mountain people grew up with a strong suspicion of outsiders. There emerged what I call a "code of the mountains." It was an unwritten code that said, "Don't trust anyone unless he is homegrown, not even preachers. And especially don't trust anything if it's labeled 'free.'" This attitude spilled over into religion. Therefore anyone who espoused a "free" salvation was suspect. My dad was one of those individuals who was suspicious.

If anyone asked my dad about accepting Christ as his personal Savior, his reply was, "When I get good enough, I will be a Christian." Now, anyone with a knowledge of the Scriptures knows that Ephesians 2:8-9, says we're saved by grace and not of work. I could not convince my dad that salvation was free until one day when the Holy Spirit intervened and showed him through a simple illustration.

I was visiting my parents which I did only a couple times a year because of distance. I shall never forget how it happened. We were standing in the kitchen, and I was going over the Gospel with Dad as I had many times before, with no results. However, this time was amazingly different.

When I witnessed to Dad I always asked him two important questions. That day was not different. "Dad," I said. "Do you know for certain that if you were to die today, you would go to heaven?"

His reply was always, "No."

Then, I would ask him a second question. "Dad, suppose you were to die today and you stood before God and He were to ask you, 'Why should I let you into my heaven?' What would you say?"

Dad's classic answer was, "When I get good enough, I will become a Christian. I'm not going to be a hypocrite."

As before, I would explain, "Heaven is a free gift. It is not earned or deserved. Man is a sinner and he cannot save himself. God is Merciful and doesn't want to punish us. But He is Just and must punish sin. Jesus, the infinite God/Man came and gave His life and purchased us a place in heaven that he offers as a free gift. And that gift is received by faith."

He listened to me as before, but I didn't see any sign of getting through to him. Then, the Holy Spirit gave me an idea. I reached into my billfold and took out a five dollar bill and said, "Dad let me illustrate the 'free gift' of eternal life to you." I handed him the five dollar bill and explained that it represented the gift of salvation.

Dad reached out and took it. When I finished explaining the Gospel, he tried to give the five dollars back to me. I refused it and explained that if I took it back, then it would not be a gift.

The illustration worked, and he prayed to trust Christ for his salvation. The light went on and it never went out. He died trusting in Christ alone for his salvation.

Two weeks before he died, Dad called me, and asked if I would preach his funeral. Of course, I agreed. He also wanted to join City Gate Church where I pastor. The church Elders and I took him in via a telephone conference call. It was the only church he ever joined

Allen Cantrell at prayer in his later days, Hamond, Kentucky

Adam

——⧫——

TODAY ADAM TOLD ME that it was his seventeenth birth-day. It didn't seem like it had been that long since I saw him in the hospital nursery struggling for his life.

Adam is my nephew and a twin. His sister, Rebecca, was born without any complications, but Adam had inhaled meconium into his lungs during delivery. Meconium is the substance that forms in the intestine during fetal development and is very irritating to the lungs if inhaled. It can cause a viral infection that can be devastating. It is usually excreted by the infant if it is under stress. This is what had happened to Adam.

As he stood there in front of me, dark, tall and handsome, just a typical teenager, my mind went back to the day I drove my brother, Michael, to the hospital to see his baby son. Adam had to be transferred immediately after his birth from Bradley County hospital in Cleveland, Tennessee, to a Chattanooga, Tennessee, hospital's intensive care unit.

I thought about the conversation Michael and I had in the car about Adam. The doctors had told Michael that Adam's condition was serious, and that he could have problems because of the meconium in his lungs. Another complication from the meconium is that it can fill up the lungs and deplete the brain of oxygen.

In an attempt to console my brother in case Adam did not survive, I said, "Michael, if God decides to take Adam He knows best. After all, that would be better than him surviving in a vegetative state."

I shall never forget Michael's response. He said, "I want Adam to live even if he is a vegetable." His statement pierced my heart, and I just knew that Adam was going to recover fully, and he did.

Adam is in high school now. He has his driver's license and owns his own car. He works and pays for his car and insurance. He is excellent with trading and handling money. His father has given him lots of liberty to flex his talent in finances. Adam has his own shop at a local flea market where he sells skateboard equipment. He is a real entrepreneur.

Last year Michael, Adam, my grandson Jonathan, and I went to Guatemala to do some mission work and enroll in Spanish language school at Centro Linguistico Maya for two weeks. We had a wonderful time. Adam is an amazing teenager.

Adam attends the church where I pastor, and I believe he is a chosen vessel of the Lord. Prayer played a crucial part in his recovery. However, I believe it was a father's love for his son that touched the heart of another Father that I know. His heart broke and bled for the well being of His Son, Jesus!

The Jesus Factor

WHEN I DO "THE MATH" Of how *Scars and Stripes* came about, it is evident that Jesus was the prime factor of the book's genesis. Everything adds up perfectly.

Years prior to my writing this book, Martha Neff and Rebecca Haskins prophesied that I would write one about my life. The first sign of her prophecy coming to pass was when Martha Neff, an Elder of City Gate Church, handed me a brochure from Waldenhouse Publishers, Inc. entitled: "Writing a book? Need help with editing...?" I contacted Karen Stone, the editor, and the rest is history.

At the first meeting with Karen, I shared with her two stories that I had written. They were "Mr. Goat" and "Picture In The Sky." She encouraged me to write a couple hundred more pages of the same and call her when I finished.

The most amazing thing happened when I came home and started writing. At the time, I had not chosen a name for the book. In fact, I had read somewhere that the name of a book should not be selected until after the manuscript was finished. Therefore, I had not even entertained a thought about what to call it. Then, a miracle happened. I dreamed one night that I was writing a book and the book was called: "Scars and Stripes." I actually woke up repeating the name of the book to myself.

Immediately, I knew that the name had been given to be supernaturally. The "Scars" referred to the many emotional scars I had suffered at the hands of an alcoholic father. The "Stripes" reminded me of the Scripture in Isaiah's prophecy about Christ's suffering: "But He was wounded for our transgressions, and He was bruised for our iniquities. The chastisement of our peace was upon Him; and with His Stripes we are healed." (Isaiah 53:5)

I called the editor and told her what had happened, and she was thrilled with the name. I was encouraged in the Lord to keep on writing.

Then, gifts from the church, family members and friends began to arrive to help cover some of the expense of publication.

Last, but by no means least, were the endorsements I received from prominent professionals in the field of Medicine, Psychiatry, and Christian Counseling.

All of the above acts of encouragement were crucial for me to continue writing, because there were many occasions when I was convinced that no one would want to read about what an adult child of an alcoholic went through. Kaye, my dear companion of forty-four years, and our two adorable children Roy (Howie) Cantrell and Karen Shaia kept encouraging me.

Most of all, I am thankful for the inspiration of my teacher, the Holy Spirit, for His inspiration and prodding to keep writing!

To God be the glory!

Hope

⟹◆⟸

I HAVE SUBTITLED THIS BOOK "Hope for adult children of alcoholic families" for one simple reason, to help the reader to see that no matter what damage is done by alcoholism in a family there is always hope.

Certainly, there are times when circumstances look hopeless. If at that juncture one throws up his hand and quits, things will not improve. However, if one will look up instead of down, during those difficult times, he will see the silver lining called hope. Hope is not found in the mud but in the stars. Hope reaches upward for the lofty heights, not downward toward the bottomless abyss. If you are presently in the basement of life, it doesn't mean you have to stay there forever. Hope is the way out.

I went to live with my parents after I graduated from high school, and there was no room for me in the house. The house was hardly livable (Mother paid $500.00 for it), but it was at least a roof over our heads. The only place for me was under the front porch. I dug out a level place for a cot and tacked up some cardboard around the sides to make a place for me to sleep. I fared well, until someone scrubbed the porch and water came through. My situation was real, and I had to live that way for a while, but hope and I knew it was only temporary.

My point is, although I lived under the front porch of our house, hope had a higher pull on me, and I knew it. My body lived under the floor, but hope lived upstairs in the house. The Good New is that hope is true to life. It strives to lift up one from the gloom, doom, and despair. Hope floats and always buoys upward. The only thing that can keep hope down is one's will and determination to give up and not try anymore.

I HOPE the following poem I wrote "lifts" your spirit.

Hope Floats

By Dr. Roy H. Cantrell
Written 6/16/05 at Destin, Florida

Hope is the wind beneath faith's wings
A force that is odorless, tasteless and never seen
Yet it is found in everyone's dreams

Hope and faith both conceived by God
But as different as two entities can be
Hope being what is envisioned
And faith what is not seen.

Hope is that inner pull toward heaven
That makes its home on cloud nine
One glimmer of its radiant grandeur
changes circumstances
In a moment of time.

Hope is what faith clings to
When substance is no where to be seen
Therefore, when faith and hope unite together
The two blend like the fragrance of spring.

Faith is more the anchor
Holding its host to the ground
Whereas hope is the air in a balloon
That lifts it heaven bound.

Faith needs hope and hope needs faith
Like two oars on a boat
When faith fails or falters
Hope floats!

About the Author

DR. ROY HAROLD CANTRELL was born in Shelby Gap, Kentucky, on August 22, 1939. He entered the ministry in 1959. Dr. Cantrell has a Doctor of Ministries degree from Christian Life School of Theology (Beacon University Institute of Ministry) and a Doctor of Philosophy in Christian Counseling from Cornerstone University. He is a licensed Pastoral Counselor with the National Christian Counselors Association, and he is a board certified substance abuse/addiction therapist, board certified integrated marriage and family therapist, and board certified temperament therapist through N.C.C.A. He is also an International Representative for them.

He has authored the following:
- *Thoughts with Meaning, Teaching Hints, Family Bible Reading, and Sentence Sermons for Teacher's Manual*
- *Keys to Camp Administration,* a manual for youth camp directors
- Numerous articles for his denomination's international magazine
- Articles for *Halo* magazine
- Article for *The Messenger*, a bimonthly publication of the National Christian Counselors Association

Dr. Cantrell is President/ Founder of City Gate Church, and serves as senior pastor. He is also Director of Beacon University Institute of Ministry, a satellite of Beacon University of Columbus,

Georgia. Dr. Cantrell is president and Founder Life Management Institute, a certified institute of the National Christian Counselors Association.

Dr. Cantrell was commissioned A KENTUCKY COLONEL by the Governor of the state of Kentucky, May, 1991. He has been involved with Evangelism Explosion for the past 25 years, serving as a certified teacher/trainer and associate clinic teacher.

He has traveled extensively, ministering in Israel, Russia, England, Mexico, Guatemala, Canada, Cyprus, Jamaica, and Cuba. His hobby is the Spanish language. He has studied Spanish at the *Centro Linguistico Maya* language school in Antigua, Guatemala.

He and his wife, Ina Kaye Goins Cantrell, pastor City Gate Church in Chattanooga, Tennessee. They have two children and five grandchildren.

What Experts Are Saying

THE POIGNANTLY TRUE STORIES In *Scars and Stripes* illuminate Dr. Cantrell's childhood experience at the hand of an alcoholic father and lend touching anecdotal evidence to the damage alcoholism can inflict upon families. As a psychologist, I have seen the effects of alcoholism on families and Dr. Cantrell's stories paint an accurate portrait of the devastation that can occur.

HE WRITES WITH INSIGHT, TENDERNESS, AND GENTLE HUMOR. The reader will be entranced by these endearing tales of a boy's heartache due to his father's alcoholism. Dr. Cantrell also shares powerful stories of his faith in God and how this faith helped him come to terms with the pain he endured as a child. Throughout the book, the reader will be deeply moved and uplifted. This book is a treasure of stories to be read again and again!

Rayna Vaught Godfrey, Ph.D.,
psychologist,
Denver, Colorado.

IT GIVES ME GREAT PLEASURE for the opportunity to endorse *Scars and Stripes.* The true stories are the embodiment of Roy's childhood experiences at the hand of an alcoholic father and a praying mother whose faith in God helped a family survive the scourge of alcoholism. The reader will be amused and amazed at the life-altering stories.

One would almost certainly agree that alcoholism rarely leaves the family without some measure of pain. As a medical doctor of more than 34 years, and having been involved every day with the effects of alcoholism and alcoholism recovery, I can attest first hand to the devastation on families. You really need to read this book if you want to learn how you can survive as an adult child of an alcoholic.

The book has been written with intelligence, insight, wit and humor at times. I think you will scarcely want to put it down once you start reading.

Ira B. Potter, M.D.

DR. CANTRELL'S BOOK *SCARS AND STRIPES* IS A "MUST" to read. It is encouraging and uplifting. His stories are "Apples of Gold." We highly recommend this book for our counselors to read for their own personal growth. We also believe that it is an excellent book for counselees to read in order to assist them as they work through the counseling process.

Drs. Richard and Phyllis Arno
Founders of National Christian
Counselors Association
Sarasota, Florida

Reference Guide

———◈———

Books:

Alcohol and Substance Abuse: A Handbook for Clergy and Congregations
Stephen P. Apthorp, Author's Choice Press, 1990, 2003.

Thirst: God and the Alcoholic
James B. Nelson, Westminster John Knox Press, 2004.

Addiction and Grace: Love and Spirituality in the Healing of Addictions
Gerald G. May, M.D., Harper San Francisco, 1991.

In Step With God: A Scriptural Guide for Practicing 12 Step Programs
Paul Barton Doyle & John Ishee, New Directions, 1990.

Love First :A New Approach to Intervention for Alcoholism and Drug Addiction
A Hazelden Guidebook
Jeff Jay & Debra Jay, Hazelden, 2004

Intervention: How to Help Someone Who Doesn't Want Help:
A Step-By-Step Guide for Families of Chemically Dependent Persons
Vernon E. Johnson, D.O., Johnson Institute/Hazelden, 1986

Links to Resources and Internet Sites:

Partnership for a Drug Free America
www.drugfreeamerica.org

American Baptist Resolution on Alcoholism and Other Chemical Dependencies
http://www.abc-usa.org/resources/resol/aicohol.htm

Core Competencies for Clergy and Other Pastoral Ministers in Addressing Alcohol and Drug Dependence and the Impact on Family Members
Substance Abuse and Mental Health Services Administration (SAMHSA)
http://www.samhsa.gov/grants/competency/

Faith: The Anti-Drug
The AntiDrug.com Resource for Faith Leaders
http://www.theantidrug.com/faith/index.asp

Faith Partners - Rush Center - Johnson Institute
http://rushcenter.org/
Trish Merrill, Director, Austin, Texas, Phone: (512) 451-9504

One Church-One Addict, Inc. (Washington, DC)
Church-Based Support Group to Assist Recovering Addicts
Contact:: Father George Clements, (202) 789-4333

Celebrate Recovery
http://www.celebraterecovery-ba.com/WhatisCR-Steps-Principles-
Parallel-3Doors.pdt

Christian Recovery International
http://www.christianrecovery.com/

**JACS: Jewish Alcoholics, Chemically Dependent Persons and
     Significant Others**
http://www.jacsweb.org/

National Association for Christian Recovery
http://www.nacronline.com/

Narcotics Anonymous - National
http://www.na.org

Alcoholics Anonymous - National and International
www.alcoholics-anonymous.orq

Cocaine Anonymous World Services
http://www.ca.org/

Dual Recovery Anonymous
http://www.draonline.org/

Al-Anon/Alateen
http://www.al-anon.alateen.org/

Alcoholics Victorious
http://av.iugm.org/

Love First Intervention
http://www.lovefirst.net/index.htm

Intervention Resource Center, Inc.
Article: Family Intervention
http://www.interventioninfo.org/research/family.asp

October Sky

WHEN I SAW THE MOVIE *OCTOBER SKY*, it was as if I had been thrust back in time, viewing my own life via "instant replay." I think seeing the movie *October Sky* will give one a better sense of the culture and a greater insight into the conditions from which *Scars & Stripes* was written.

October Sky is a true story of Homer Hickman, a coal miner's son who was inspired by the launching of the Russian Satellite, Sputnik (October 4, 1957), to experiment with rocketry. His father, John Hickman (played by Chris Cooper), wanted his son to be a miner like himself. The story is framed around a little mining community called Coalwood, West Virginia, less than 10 miles from where I grew up in Newhall.

Our lives parallel in many ways:

- We lived in the same county and state of Welch, West Virginia.

- We attended the same high school at War, West Virginia. (Big Creek high school) the same year (1957).

- Our fathers were coal miners.

- Our mothers played a huge role in each of our lives. They didn't want us to end up in the coal mines.

- Our mothers wanted us to get an education and our father didn't.

- We went to college. Homer became an engineer with NASA and a successful author, and I became a minister and author. Going to college was something unusual in coal country at the time.

Quentin Wilson (Played by Chris Owens) is my favorite character in the movie. Quentin was very poor and so was I. The scene in the movie that touched me the most is when Homer went to Quentin's house late one night to ask him for help to solve a math problem. Quentin's house was located in the slum part of town. As Homer was leaving, Quentin asked him not to tell anyone where he lived. I could relate to Quentin's concern about his peers knowing where he lived because people can be cruel at times. I lived with the same dread of people knowing where I lived, or who my alcoholic father was.

I love the tagline of the movie: "Sometimes one dream is enough to light up the whole sky." My dream is that *Scars & Stripes*, will light up your sky and give you hope for the future because God has a plan for your life.

Note: Ironically, in the steam engine scene where the "rocket boys" are salvaging scarp iron from unused railroad tracts, the Norfolk and Western coal hauling steam engine they see is the former Southern Railway locomotive # 4501. The engine is currently in use at the Tennessee Valley Railroad Museum in Chattanooga, Tennessee, where I now live.

October Sky is rated PG for language, brief teen sensuality and alcohol use, and for some thematic elements.

The Simple ABC'S of Salvation

A   **ADMIT** that you are a sinner (Romans 3:23)

B   **BELIEVE** that Jesus died and arose from the grave to purchase you a place in heaven that He offers as a free gift. (Roman 6:23 and Ephesians 2:8, 9)

C   **CONFESS** your sins to Christ who is "faithful and just to forgive us ours sins and to cleanse us from all unrighteousness." (I John 1:9)

Pray This Prayer

"Lord Jesus, I admit that I am a sinner. I believe that you died on the cross to purchase me a place in heaven that you offer as a free gift. I confess that I have sinned against You, and am not worthy of this gift. You promised in Revelation 3 :20 that if I would open the door to my heart, confess my sins, and invite You into my heart, You would make me a part of your family. In Jesus name, I open my heart and invite You to come in. I ask for forgiveness of my sins. I transfer my faith from my good works and myself to You alone for my salvation. I receive You as the resurrected and living Christ, and as my Lord and Savior. Amen"

My Commitment

Now that I have received the gift of eternal life, and know that I am your child, I commit my life to you to...

D   **DO** all that you command me to do. I further commit to…
Prayer
Bible Study
Share my testimony with others.
Fellowship with other believers (Hebrews 10:25)
Worship

Contact Me

If you prayed this prayer and believe that Jesus came into your heart, contact me at:
www.scarsandstripes.org

TO ORDER MORE COPIES OF *SCARS & STRIPES*

Online: go to www.scarsandstripes.org
By Mail: Send a copy of this order form with a check payable to
Dr. Roy H. Cantrell, 6947 Hickory View Ln., Chattanooga, TN 37421

Name: _____

Ship to: _____

_____

City_____ St/Prov_____ Zip_____

Quantity _____@ $14.95 US $19.44 Can $_____

      TN residents add $1.46 tax per book $_____

      Shipping add $3.85 one book $_____

      Add $1.50 shipping each additional book $_____

TOTAL amount enclosed $_____

— — — — — — — — — — — — — — — — —

TO ORDER MORE COPIES OF *SCARS & STRIPES*

Online: go to scarsandstripes.org
By Mail: Send a copy of this order form with a check payable to
Dr. Roy H. Cantrell, 6947 Hickory View Ln., Chattanooga, TN 37421

Name: _____

Ship to: _____

_____

City_____ St/Prov_____ Zip_____

Quantity _____@ $14.95 US $19.44 Can $_____

      TN residents add $ 1.46 tax per book $_____

      Shipping add $3.85 one book $_____

      Add $1.50 shipping each additional book $_____

TOTAL amount enclosed $_____

Type and design by Karen Paul Stone
Myriad on Husky 50# white